# ON KILLING

# ON KILLING
## MEDITATIONS ON
## THE CHASE

*Edited and*
*with an Introduction by*
ROBERT F. JONES

The Lyons Press
Guilford, Connecticut
An imprint of The Globe Pequot Press

The Lyons Press is an imprint of The Globe Pequot Press.

Printed in the United States of America

2 4 6 8 10 9 7 5 3 1

The Library of Congress Cataloging-in-Publication Data is available on file.

Permissions Acknowledgments

From *For Whom the Bell Tolls* by Ernest Hemingway, copyright ©1940 by Ernest Hemingway. Reprinted with the permission of Scribner, a division of Simon & Schuster, Inc. and Ernest Hemingway Rights Trust.

From *All Quiet on the Western Front* by Erich Maria Remarque. "Im Westen Nichts Neues," copyright © 1928 by Ullstein A.G.; copyright renewed © 1956 by Erich Maria Remarque. "All Quiet on the Western Front," copyright © 1929, 1930 by Little, Brown & Company; copyright renewed 1957, 1958 by Erich Maria Remarque. All rights reserved.

"Thinking Like a Mountain," from *A Sand County Almanac: And Sketches Here and There* by Aldo Leopold, copyright © 1949, 1977 by Oxford University Press, Inc. Used by permission of Oxford University Press.

"A Few Thoughts on Adam's Curse," copyright © 2001 by Dan Gerber. All rights reserved.

From *Farmer* by Jim Harrison, copyright © 1976 by Jim Harrison. Reprinted by permission of the author.

"A Question of Blessings," copyright © 2001 by Robert F. Jones. All rights reserved.

"Bambi and Lassie," copyright © 2001 by Mary Clearman Blew. All rights reserved.

"Putting Fish Back," from *Fisherman's Spring* by Roderick Haig-Brown, copyright © 1951, 1975 by Roderick Haig-Brown.

"Death on the Musselshell," copyright © 2001 by John Holt. All rights reserved.

From *Out of Africa* by Isak Dinesen, copyright © 1937 by Random House, Inc. and renewed 1965 by Rungstedlundfonden. Used by permission of Random House, Inc.

"Predilections," copyright © 2001 by Le Anne Schreiber. All rights reserved.

"My War on *Marmota Monax*," copyright © 2001 by Louise Jones. All rights reserved.

"Praise God for the Blood of the Bull," from *West With the Night* by Beryl Markham, copyright © 1942, 1983 by Beryl Markham. Used by permission of Farrar, Straus & Giroux Inc.

"Sheep Hunting, with Oil Man John," copyright © 2001 by Pam Houston. All rights reserved.

"Heart of the Hunt," copyright © 2001 by Allen Morris Jones. All rights reserved.

"Killing the Neural Pathways," copyright © 2001 by John Jerome. All rights reserved.

"The Hunter's Dance," copyright © 2001 by Louis Owens. All rights reserved.

"Meat," from *On the Edge of the Wild* by Stephen J. Bodio, copyright © 1998 by Stephen J. Bodio. Reprinted with the permission of the Lyons Press.

"The Pipal Pani Tiger," from *Man-Eaters of Kumaon* by Jim Corbett, reproduced by permission of Oxford University Press, New Delhi, India.

"Communion," copyright © 2001 by Dan O'Brien. All rights reserved.

"Thoughts on Killing," from *The Upland Equation* by Charles Fergus, copyright © 1995 by Charles Fergus. Reprinted with the permission of the Lyons Press.

*One does not hunt in order to kill; on the contrary, one kills in order to have hunted.*

—José Ortega y Gassett
<small>MEDITATIONS ON HUNTING (1942)</small>

# CONTENTS

Introduction                                 Robert F. Jones         1

*Part One*

From FOR WHOM THE BELL TOLLS               Ernest Hemingway     13

From ALL QUIET ON THE WESTERN FRONT    Erich Maria Remarque    19

*Part Two*

THE PASSENGER PIGEON                    John James Audubon     29

(from *Ornithological Biographies*)

THINKING LIKE A MOUNTAIN              Aldo Leopold         37

(from *Sand County Almanac*)

*Part Three*

A FEW THOUGHTS ON ADAM'S CURSE      Dan Gerber           43

From FARMER                                Jim Harrison         49

A QUESTION OF BLESSINGS                Robert F. Jones       55

*Part Four*

From ANNA KARENINA                      Leo Tolstoy          69

BAMBI AND LASSIE                     Mary Clearman Blew     75

*Part Five*

PUTTING FISH BACK                    Roderick Haig-Brown    87

(from *Fisherman's Spring*)

DEATH ON THE MUSSELSHELL          John Holt           95

# Contents

*Part Six*
From OUT OF AFRICA     Isak Dinesen     105
PREDILECTIONS     Le Anne Schreiber     115
MY WAR ON MARMOTA MONAX     Louise Jones     123

*Part Seven*
PRAISE GOD FOR THE BLOOD OF THE BULL     Beryl Markham     131
    (from *West with the Night*)
SHEEP HUNTING WITH OIL MAN JOHN     Pam Houston     153
HEART OF THE HUNT     Allen Morris Jones     165

*Part Eight*
ONE DAY NEAR MARILAL     Dan Gerber     175
    (from *Trying to Catch the Horses*)
KILLING THE NEURAL PATHWAYS     John Jerome     177
THE HUNTER'S DANCE     Louis Owens     183
MEAT (from *The Edge of Wild*)     Stephen J. Bodio     195
THE PIPAL PANI TIGER     Jim Corbett     211
    (from *Man-Eaters of Kumaon*)

*Part Nine*
COMMUNION     Dan O'Brien     225
THOUGHTS ON KILLING     Charles Fergus     233
    (from *The Upland Equation*)

Contributors     237

# ON KILLING

# INTRODUCTION

*Man is man, and not a chimpanzee, because for millions upon millions of evolving years we killed for a living. If among all the members of our primate family the human being is unique, even in our noblest aspirations, it is because we alone through untold millions of years were continuously dependent on killing to survive.*

—Robert Ardrey
THE HUNTING HYPOTHESIS (1976)

*Every good hunter is uneasy in the depths of his conscience when faced with the death he is about to inflict on the enchanting animal.*

—José Ortega y Gassett
MEDITATIONS ON HUNTING (1942)

KILLING ANYTHING, man or bird, fish or mammal, is a most memorable act. Perhaps that's why hunters and fishermen, and soldiers especially, can describe to the last detail the conditions that prevailed at the moment of their kills: weather, wind direction, cloud cover or lack of it, date, time of day, the way the light played on water or feather, fur or fin or enemy helmet.

Conflicted as they often are, feelings about killing are harder to describe. Too often we fall back lamely on mere narrative.

*1*

The first warm-blooded creature I killed, I'm sorry to admit, was a songbird. It was April 12, 1945, a cold, blustery spring afternoon in Wauwatosa, Wisconsin, and I was ten years old. My friend Donny Caswell had received a BB gun for his birthday—a Daisy Red Ryder Special. We were plinking away at various targets in the empty field beside his house, but not hitting many. Tin cans, an orange crate, an empty Quaker Oats container that had blown out of someone's trash can, even the coalchunk eyes of a melting snowman in a neighbor's backyard. Then a robin alighted on a leafless bush. It was maybe twenty yards away. Never thinking for a moment that I would or even could hit it, I popped off a shot at this plump, chirpy harbinger of spring, and—to my horror—it fell.

Robin Redbreast was dead!

We were appalled. I'd been fishing since before I could remember, but the death of a scaled, spiky, cold-blooded water-breather was nothing compared to this.

At that very moment Donny's mother opened the kitchen window, leaned out, and yelled for us to get in there. *Quick!* Her face was pale with shock. Thinking we were really in for it now, and deservedly so, we dragged our feet and sorry butts into the kitchen where the radio was playing what sounded like funeral music. "Boys, I hate to tell you," Mrs. Caswell said, and tears spilled down her cheeks. "Our President is dead, I just heard it on WTMJ."

My first thought was: God's Retribution! President Roosevelt is dead because I killed that robin! Without him we'll certainly lose the war!

You'd think that incident would have put me off guns and hunting for life, but three years later I acquired a shotgun. In the company of a pair of neighborhood Irish Setters who had nothing better to do, I began seriously hunting and—later, when I'd learned to outsmart the birds (not ever easy)—actually killing and eating the prairie chickens, pheasants, grouse and woodcock that abounded on the remnant of native prairie across the road from my house or in the riverine woods nearby. I've been a seasonal predator ever since, but never without a twinge of remorse in my heart for the birds, fish, and animals I've killed. Of course we didn't lose World War II, and I no longer think that my random shot at that innocent robin killed FDR, not even figuratively. But I remember the moment—and the man—with every bird I drop.

For an animal that evolved over millions of years as a tough, clumsy, weak-muscled, hard-eyed, bipedal killer, we are remarkably reluctant to discuss our most distinguishing characteristic in a straightforward manner. There seems to be a reluctance to view ourselves as killers. The aim of this book is to examine how such thoughts and feelings have come to bear on one of mankind's oldest means of survival: The Chase, whether it be for wild game or wild fish. In essence, hunting and fishing are really the same activity—the intense, hot-blooded, clear-eyed pursuit of wild quarry, though with different tools in different mediums. But the aim in all cases is to kill what we seek.

Our contemporary English word "kill" stems from the Middle English *killen* by way of the Old English *cyllan,* and it in turn from the Germanic *kuljan.* All derive from a Proto-Indo-European root *gwel*(2)—which means to pierce, quell, destroy, kill. Another related root, *gwel*(1), means to throw, from which we get our modern word "ball," as in cannonball, musket ball, or bullet. Throw a stone or a spear, shoot an arrow or a bullet, and pierce an animal, thus quelling its life. Though there are other, more advanced ways of doing it—from deployment of rat traps, nets, and deadfalls to poison gases, bombs, rockets, or thermonuclear blasts—that's basically what killing means.

Still, in our uneasiness with the whole idea, we tend to employ certain diversionary euphemisms in discussing the "killing" of animals, fish or birds, i.e. innocent creatures: we collect them, harvest them, we dispatch, drop, bag, pot, or pop them, we cull or reduce the size of their herds, we down them or put them down, often we gather them (as in "I guess I'll wander out on the moor, m'dear, and see if I can't gather a few partridge, perhaps collect a hare or two for the pot."). Once the creature is within our grasp, we deliver the coup de grace, put out its lights, or simply knock it on the head.

Harsher euphemisms, oddly enough, are often applied to the killing of human beings, perhaps implying that they're getting what they deserve: laconic, metaphorical, tough, unfeeling terms, even witty in some cases. We scrag them, snuff, mow down, blow away, off, rub out, or ventilate them, in order to let in some doubtless well-earned daylight; in other cases we cancel his or her ticket, waste an unworthy fellow (or lady), light up a third, wipe out a fourth, or—one of my favorites—terminate him or her with extreme prejudice.

Genesis, verse 28. God to Adam: "Be fruitful and multiply, and replenish the earth, and subdue it: and have dominion over the fish of the sea, and over the fowl of the air, and over every living thing that moveth upon the earth."

Exodus, Chapter I. God to Moses: "Thou shalt not kill."

Do we sense a conflict here?

Anyone capable of reading this book at the time of its publication was necessarily born in the twentieth century—the deadliest hundred years in human history. The Killing Time. Our two World Wars killed at least 60 million people, military and civilian alike. Lesser conflicts like Korea, Vietnam and the Gulf War upped that toll by a million or more. Minor-scale civil wars, coups d'états, rebellions, and insurrections across the planet from Chechnya to Africa to East Asia, the Middle East, Afghanistan, Latin America to the Balkans, including the genocides, purges, and "ethnic cleansings" from Armenia in the 1920s, to Hitler's death camps, to Stalin's Gulag, Pol Pot's Cambodia, and Maoist China, to the present-day Balkans, not to mention the ongoing slaughters in sub-Saharan Africa—Rwanda, the southern Sudan, Somalia and Ethiopia, Uganda, much of Central Africa, and Mozambique—added millions more. According to some authorities, a mind-boggling total of 169 million human beings have been killed by others of their species in the twentieth century. These murderous spasms killed not only people, but their murderous side-effects also cut deeply into all species of life on the planet. Yet human population continues to grow apace.

It's too easy merely to lament these losses, even to write outraged essays or pathetic lyrics about them, and thus feel righteous for being on God's or Nature's or the politically correct side. The problem is graver than that. Scientists believe there have been five "major extinction spasms" on the planet over the course of the 3.5 billion years since life began. These great setbacks to evolution, one of which (at the end of the Paleozoic era some 245 million years ago) wiped out 96 percent of the earth's sea-dwelling species along with the dinosaurs that dominated the land, were caused by natural phenomena: meteor impacts and/or climate changes.

Edward O. Wilson, the Pulitzer-prize-winning Harvard scientist who is one of the world's leading authorities on everything from the lives of the ants to the death of nature, believes we are now in the midst of the sixth such spasm—this one attributable entirely to man. In *The Diversity of Life* (Cambridge, MA: Harvard University Press, 1992), Wilson describes how human population pressures, particularly in the developing nations of the Third World, are destroying other species of life at a disastrous rate. Human beings are

overwhelming nature. By the year 2020—less than a human generation from now—no fewer than 20 percent of the earth's currently
existing species of plants and animals will be extinct, by Wilson's
conservative estimate.

No one knows with anything like certainty just how many
species—from microbes and molds through insects and flowers to
gamebirds and deer and trout, eagles and elephants and whales—
there are on our once-green and rich planet. Estimates range from
ten million to as high as a hundred million. Tropical forests contain
more than half the species of life on earth, and already half of those
fecund woodlands have been cut down for human use. Exotic hardwoods have been harvested—from Southeast Asia to Africa to South
and Central America—to panel posh homes and offices from Tokyo
to Manhattan to Oslo. The grain fields and grazing lands that replace
the forests will erode in a generation or two, leaving bare lifeless
bedrock in its wake. By 2020, even the woodlands that remain—some
eight million square kilometers—will be cut in half again, or perhaps
by as much as 70 percent. Wilson estimates, again conservatively, that
because of this runaway destruction of the earth's tropical forests, the
planet is losing twenty-seven thousand species a year: seventy-four a
day, or a little more than three species an hour (even while we sleep,
and even if we don't own a gun or have never plied a fishing rod).

And extinction is forever.

Little wonder, then, that the simple word "killing" has become to
many an obscenity. Despite Jehovah's biblical grant to Adam and his
descendants of "dominion" over all living creatures, many people
want to see hunting and even fishing outlawed. God's marching or-
ders seem to them entirely wrong-headed.

Yet we have to kill in order to eat—if not red meat or fish or
fowl, then anyway at least the plants that can sustain our protein-

based life forms. Soybeans and rice and yams and plantains and apples and spinach and the great harvest of those "amber waves of grain" famed in song and story: wheat, rye, bulgur, sorghum, and corn. Even seaweed is on today's human menu—all that's even remotely edible must die and go into our bellies in order to fulfill God's first order to Adam—"Be fruitful and multiply, and fill the earth. . . ." Death makes life. Even in drinking a glass of "pure" water, we are killing hundreds, perhaps millions, of harmless microscopic life forms. But some of them, not surprisingly, have their own survival strategies, like amoebic dysentery, bilharzia and giardia, commonly known as "beaver fever," which can sicken or even kill us.

In the nineteenth century a notion grew up among thoughtful, well-meaning, soul-searching people that led to a concept called "Breathe-Airianism." The idea was that by not eating or drinking anything at all, one could sustain life in full, good health simply by inhaling, regularly and rhythmically of course, God's pure, sweet, fresh, life-sustaining air. In the process not a single living creature, plant or animal, would come to harm. But alas there is little food value in air, as serious Breathe-Airians soon discovered, and even the purest breath of it contains tiny living creatures, many of which are only waiting a chance to enter a dark, warm, humid environment like a human lung to go about their own business of killing and eating. Hence many of mankind's most troublesome afflictions from the common cold, measles, and tuberculosis, to Ebola, Legionnaire's disease, Hanta Virus, and much more.

A dog-eat-dog world indeed. Or perhaps a bug-eat-man one.

The scope of this anthology is an examination of these contradictions as they bear on hunting and fishing, expressed in the works of various respected writers and thinkers, both those of the past and our own contemporaries. My aim has been to limit these essays and snippets of fiction to the traditional "blood sports." But considering the fact that many anti-hunters today simplistically liken that sport to war, I felt it instructive to include brief excerpts from two of the past century's most celebrated war novels: Ernest Hemingway's *For Whom the Bell Tolls* and Erich Maria Remarque's *All Quiet on the Western Front.* Hemingway's passage discusses in brief, humorous dialogue the difference of opinion between an intellectual American volunteer, Robert Jordan, and his peasant guide, a soft-hearted hunter named Anselmo, on a guerrilla mission during the Spanish Civil War. They disagree, in a genteel, Cervantes-like way, about the propriety of killing men as opposed to animals.

Grimmer by far, Remarque's excerpt concerns a ghastly rendezvous in a shell-hole in No-Man's-Land between a young German infantryman, Paul Baumer, and a middle-aged French *poilu,* who unfortunately stumble into the same shelter at the same moment during an artillery barrage. Baumer in panic sticks a trench knife into the Frenchman's chest. But the *poilu* does not go gentle into that good night. . . . I first read this passage when I was fourteen years old and had just begun hunting. The images it evoked have remained with me all these years, and to some degree or another they've colored my emotions whenever I've hooked a fish, shot a bird, or sent a rifle bullet through the shoulder or heart of a big game animal.

The balance of the pieces in this book range from out-and-out disavowal or condemnation of killing other creatures (Le Anne Schreiber, Dan Gerber, and John Jerome), to expressions of elation in the hunt and its culminating act (Isak Dinesen, Beryl Markham).

Others express the ambivalence that even the most dedicated hunter—or home gardener for that matter—feels at terminating the life of another living entity (Jim Harrison, Jim Corbett, Louise Jones).

Some of the writers, like Charles Fergus and the late José Ortega y Gassett, address the ethical questions and dilemmas raised by killing. A little-known excerpt from Leo Tolstoy's *Anna Karenina* and Dan O'Brien's original essay show how hunters relate to the "lesser creatures" that aid and abet them in the chase—their dogs and their hawks.

Essays by Louis Owens and Steven J. Bodio clash on the seemingly simple question of meat-eating, not over dietary considerations but rather the preference for store-bought or wild meat.

As a hunting guide in Alaska, Pam Houston had come to feel that most of her clients were rich, spoiled, and morally suspect—"trophy hunters" in the worst sense of the phrase, seeking only the bragging rights to big heads and horns, while she did most of the real work. She was in for a surprise. Her graphic, sensitive account of a successful Dall sheep hunt describes her discovery of what to her seemed a very rare thing: a Good Hunter.

Too bad she hadn't already met Allen Morris Jones, whose first-person narrative of a bow-hunt for elk in the Missouri Breaks of Montana shows ethical hunting at its best, down to last grave, respectful detail of dressing out his kill.

Two eminent fishing writers, John Holt and the late Roderick Haig-Brown, bring the discussion of killing to bear on the practice of "catch-and-release."

Aldo Leopold, a lifelong hunter and a major figure in American conservation who died more than half a century ago, prefigures and complements Mary Clearman Blew on the question of what to kill and when (if ever) to kill it.

No discussion of killing would be complete without some words from that great killer/artist John James Audubon (1785–1851), who slew thousands of birds and mammals to give us his beautiful wildlife paintings. He worked in an era before cameras, so he was necessarily a killer in order to fulfill his art—though in many cases a reluctant one. If ambivalence about killing is the inarticulate major premise of this book, Audubon's essay on "The Passenger Pigeon" is its best exemplar, a worthy companion to his portrait of that wild, doomed, beautiful bird.

All of these essays and stories, regardless of the position taken by their authors, are heartfelt and well-written. Taken together, I hope, they might help to clarify our dual role as predators and as lovers of what remains wild—both in nature and in our own hearts.

—*Robert F. Jones*

# Part One

From

# FOR WHOM THE BELL TOLLS

### Ernest Hemingway

"LET US GO," Robert Jordan said. He started up the hill, moving carefully and taking advantage of the cover until they were out of sight. Anselmo followed him at a hundred yards distance. When they were well out of sight of the bridge, he stopped and the old man came up and went into the lead and climbed steadily through the pass, up the steep slope in the dark.

"We have a formidable aviation," the old man said happily.

"Yes."

"And we will win."

"We have to win."

"Yes. And after we have won you must come to hunt."

"To hunt what?"

"The boar, the bear, the wolf, the ibex—"

"You like to hunt?"

"Yes, man. More than anything. We all hunt in my village. You do not like to hunt?"

"No," said Robert Jordan. "I do not like to kill animals."

"With me it is the opposite," the old man said. "I do not like to kill men."

"Nobody does except those who are disturbed in the head," Robert Jordan said. "But I feel nothing against it when it is necessary. When it is for the cause."

"It is a different thing, though," Anselmo said. "In my house, when I had a house, and now I have no house, there were the tusks of boar I had shot in the lower forest. There were the hides of wolves I had shot. In the winter, hunting them in the snow. One very big one, I killed at dusk in the outskirts of the village on my way home one night in November. There were four wolf hides on the floor of my house. They were worn by stepping on them but they were wolf hides. There were the horns of ibex that I had killed in the high Sierra, and there was an eagle stuffed by an embalmer of birds of Avila, with his wings spread, and eyes as yellow and real as the eyes of an eagle alive. It was a very beautiful thing and all of those things gave me great pleasure to contemplate."

"Yes," said Robert Jordan.

"On the door of the church of my village was nailed the paw of a bear that I killed in the spring, finding him on a hillside in the snow, overturning a log with this same paw."

"When was this?"

"Six years ago. And every time I saw that paw, like the hand of a man, but with those long claws, dried and nailed through the palm to the door of the church, I received a pleasure."

"Of pride?"

"Of pride of remembrance of the encounter with the bear on that hillside in the early spring. But of the killing of a man, who is a man as we are, there is nothing good that remains."

"You can't nail his paw to the church," Robert Jordan said.

"No. Such a barbarity is unthinkable. Yet the hand of a man is like the paw of a bear."

"So is the chest of a man like the chest of a bear," Robert Jordan said. "With the hide removed from the bear, there are many similarities in the muscles."

"Yes," Anselmo said. "The gypsies believe the bear to be a brother of man."

"So do the Indians in America," Robert Jordan said. "And when they kill a bear they apologize to him and ask his pardon. They put his skull in a tree and they ask him to forgive them before they leave it."

"The gypsies believe the bear to be a brother to man because he has the same body beneath his hide, because he drinks beer, because he enjoys music and because he likes to dance."

"So also believe the Indians."

"Are the Indians then gypsies?"

"No. But they believe alike about the bear."

"Clearly. The gypsies also believe he is a brother because he steals for pleasure."

"Have you gypsy blood?"

"No. But I have seen much of them and clearly, since the movement, more. There are many in the hills. To them it is not a sin to kill outside the tribe. They deny this but it is true."

"Like the Moors."

"Yes. But the gypsies have many laws they do not admit to having. In the war many gypsies have become bad again as they were in the olden times."

"They do not understand why the war is made. They do not know for what we fight."

"No," Anselmo said. "They only know now there is a war and people may kill again as in the olden times without a surety of punishment."

"You have killed?" Robert Jordan asked in the intimacy of the dark and of their day together.

"Yes. Several times. But not with pleasure. To me it is a sin to kill a man. Even Fascists whom we must kill. To me there is a great difference between the bear and the man and I do not believe the wizardry of the gypsies about the brotherhood with animals. No. I am against all killing of men."

"Yet you have killed."

"Yes. And will again. But if I live later, I will try to live in such a way, doing no harm to any one, that it will be forgiven."

"By whom?"

"Who knows? Since we do not have God here any more, neither His Son nor the Holy Ghost, who forgives? I do not know."

"You have not God any more?"

"No. Man. Certainly not. If there were God, never would He have permitted what I have seen with my eyes. Let *them* have God."

"They claim Him."

"Clearly I miss Him, having been brought up in religion. But now a man must be responsible to himself."

"Then it is thyself who will forgive thee for killing."

"I believe so," Anselmo said. "Since you put it clearly in that way I believe that must be it. But with or without God, I think it is a sin to kill. To take the life of another is to me very grave. I will do it whenever necessary but I am not of the race of Pablo."

"To win a war we must kill our enemies. That has always been true."

"Clearly. In war we must kill. But I have very rare ideas," Anselmo said.

They were walking now close together in the dark and he spoke softly, sometimes turning his head as he climbed. "I would not kill even a Bishop. I would not kill a proprietor of any kind. I would make them work each day as we have worked in the fields and as we work in the mountains with the timber, all of the rest of their lives. So they would see what man is born to. That they should sleep where we sleep. That they should eat as we eat. But above all that they should work. Thus they would learn."

"And they would survive to enslave thee again."

From

# ALL QUIET ON THE WESTERN FRONT

### Erich Maria Remarque

ALREADY IT HAS become somewhat lighter. Steps hasten over me. The first. Gone. Again, another. The rattle of machine-guns becomes an unbroken chain. Just as I am about to turn round a little, something heavy stumbles, and with a crash a body falls over me into the shell-hole, slips down, and lies across me—

I do not think at all, I make no decision—I strike madly at home, and feel only how the body suddenly convulses, then becomes limp, and collapses. When I recover myself, my hand is sticky and wet.

The man gurgles. It sounds to me as though he bellows, every gasping breath is like a cry, a thunder—but it is not only my heart pounding. I want to stop his mouth, stuff it with earth, stab him again, he must be quiet, he is betraying me; now at last I regain control of myself, but have suddenly become so feeble that I cannot any more lift my hand against him.

So I crawl away to the farthest corner and stay there, my eyes glued on him, my hand grasping the knife—ready, if he stirs, to

*19*

spring at him again. But he won't do so any more, I can hear that already in his gurgling.

I can see him indistinctly. I have but one desire, to get away. If it is not soon it will be too light; it will be difficult enough now. Then as I try to raise up my head I see it is impossible already. The machine-gunfire so sweeps the ground that I should be shot through and through before I could make one jump.

I test it once with my helmet, which I take off and hold up to find out the level of the shots. The next moment it is knocked out of my hand by a bullet. The fire is sweeping very low to the ground. I am not far enough from the enemy line to escape being picked off by one of the snipers if I attempt to get away.

The light increases. Burning I wait for our attack. My hands are white at the knuckles, I clench them so tightly in my longing for the fire to cease so that my comrades may come.

Minute after minute trickles away. I dare not look again at the dark figure in the shell-hole. With an effort I look past it and wait, wait. The bullets hiss, they make a steel net, never ceasing, never ceasing.

Then I notice my bloody hand and suddenly feel nauseated. I take some earth and rub the skin with it; now my hand is muddy and the blood cannot be seen any more.

The fire does not diminish. It is equally heavy from both sides. Our fellows have probably given me up for lost long ago.

It is early morning, clear and gray. The gurgling continues, I stop my ears, but soon take my fingers away again, because then I cannot hear the other sound.

The figure opposite me moves. I shrink together and involuntarily look at it. Then my eyes remain glued to it. A man with a small pointed beard lies there; his head is fallen to one side, one arm is halfbent, his head rests helplessly upon it. The other hand lies on his chest, it is bloody.

He is dead, I say to myself, he must be dead, he doesn't feel anything any more; it is only the body that is gurgling there. Then the head tries to raise itself, for a moment the groaning becomes louder, his forehead sinks back upon his arm. The man is not dead, he is dying, but he is not dead. I drag myself toward him, hesitate, support myself on my hands, creep a bit farther, wait, again a terrible journey. At last I am beside him.

Then he opens his eyes. He must have heard me, for he gazes at me with a look of utter terror. The body lies still, but in the eyes there is such an extraordinary expression of fright that for a moment I think they have power enough to carry the body off with them. Hundreds of miles away with one bound. The body is still perfectly still, without a sound, the gurgle has ceased, but the eyes cry out, yell, all the life is gathered together in them for one tremendous effort to flee, gathered together there in a dreadful terror of death, of me.

My legs give way and I drop on my elbows. "No, no," I whisper.

The eyes follow me. I am powerless to move so long as they are there.

Then his hand slips slowly from his breast, only a little bit, it sinks just a few inches, but this movement breaks the power of the eyes. I bend forward, shake my head and whisper: "No, no, no," I raise one hand, I must show him that I want to help him, I stroke his forehead.

The eyes shrink back as the hand comes, then they lose their stare, the eyelids droop lower, the tension is past. I open his collar and place his head more comfortably.

His mouth stands half open, it tries to form words. The lips are dry. My water bottle is not there. I have not brought it with me. But there is water in the mud, down at the bottom of the crater. I climb down, take out my handkerchief, spread it out, push it under and scoop up the yellow water that strains through into the hollow of my hand.

He gulps it down. I fetch some more. Then I unbutton his tunic in order to bandage him if it is possible. In any case I must do it, so that if the fellows over there capture me they will see that I wanted to help him, and so will not shoot me. He tries to resist, but his hand is too feeble. The shirt is stuck and will not come away, it is buttoned at the back. So there is nothing for it but to cut it open.

I look for the knife and find it again. But when I begin to cut the shirt the eyes open once more and the cry is in them again and the demented expression, so that I must close them, press them shut and whisper: "I want to help you, Comrade, camerade, camerade, camerade—" eagerly repeating the word, to make him understand.

There are three stabs. My field dressing covers them, the blood runs out under it, I press it tighter; there; he groans.

That is all I can do. Now we must wait, wait.

These hours. . . . The gurgling starts again—but how slowly a man dies! For this I know—he cannot be saved, I have, indeed, tried to tell myself that he will be, but at noon this pretence breaks down and melts before his groans. If only I had not lost my revolver crawling about, I would shoot him. Stab him I cannot.

By noon I am groping on the outer limits of reason. Hunger devours me, I could almost weep for something to eat, I cannot struggle against it. Again and again I fetch water for the dying man and drink some myself.

This is the first time I have killed with my hands, whom I can see close at hand, whose death is my doing. Kat and Kropp and Müller have experienced it already, when they have hit someone; it happens to many, in hand-to-hand fighting especially—

But every gasp lays my heart bare. This dying man has time with him, he has an invisible dagger with which he stabs me: Time and my thoughts.

I would give much if he would but stay alive. It is hard to lie here and to have to see and hear him.

In the afternoon, about three, he is dead.

I breathe freely again. But only for a short time. Soon the silence is more unbearable than the groans. I wish the gurgling were there again, gasping hoarse, now whistling softly and again hoarse and loud.

It is mad, what I do. But I must do something. I prop the dead man up again so that he lies comfortably, although he feels nothing any more. I close his eyes. They are brown, his hair is black and a bit curly at the sides.

The mouth is full and soft beneath his moustache; the nose is slightly arched, the skin brownish; it is now not so pale as it was before, when he was still alive. For a moment the face seems almost healthy;—then it collapses suddenly into the strange face of the dead that I have so often seen, strange faces, all alike.

No doubt his wife still thinks of him; she does not know what happened. He looks as if he would have often written to her;—she will still be getting mail from him—To-morrow, in a week's time—perhaps even a stray letter a month hence. She will read it, and in it he will be speaking to her.

My state is getting worse, I can no longer control my thoughts. What would his wife look like? Like the little brunette on the other side of the canal? Does she belong to me now? Perhaps by this act she becomes mine. I wish Kantorek were sitting here beside me. If my mother could see me—. The dead man might have had thirty more years of life if only I had impressed the way back to our trench more sharply on my memory. If only he had run two yards farther to

23

the left, he might now be sitting in the trench over there and writing a fresh letter to his wife.

But I will get no further that way; for that is the fate of all of us: if Kemmerich's leg had been six inches to the right: if Haie Westhus had bent his back three inches further forward—

The silence spreads. I talk and must talk. So I speak to him and to say to him: "Comrade, I did not want to kill you. If you jumped in here again, I would not do it, if you would be sensible too. But you were only an idea to me before, an abstraction that lived in my mind and called forth its appropriate response. It was that abstraction I stabbed. But now, for the first time, I see you are a man like me. I thought of your hand-grenades, of your bayonet, of your rifle; now I see your wife and your face and our fellowship. Forgive me, comrade. We always see it too late. Why do they never tell us that you are poor devils like us, that your mothers are just as anxious as ours, and that we have the same fear of death, and the same dying and the same agony—Forgive me, comrade; how could you be my enemy? If we threw away these rifles and this uniform you could be my brother just like Kat and Albert. Take twenty years of my life, comrade, and stand up—take more, for I do not know what I can even attempt to do with it now."

It is quiet, the front is still except for the crackle of rifle fire. The bullets rain over, they are not fired haphazard, but shrewdly aimed from all sides. I cannot get out.

"I will write to your wife," I say hastily to the dead man, "I will write to her, she must hear it from me, I will tell her everything I have told you, she shall not suffer, I will help her, and your parents too, and your child—"

His tunic is half open. The pocket-book is easy to find. But I hesitate to open it. In it is the book with his name. So long as I do not know his name perhaps I may still forget him, time will obliterate it, this picture. But his name, it is a nail that will be hammered into me and never come out again. It has the power to recall this forever, it will always come back and stand before me.

Irresolutely I take the wallet in my hand. It slips out of my hand and falls open. Some pictures and letters drop out. I gather them up and want to put them back again, but the strain I am under, the uncertainty, the hunger, the danger, these hours with the dead man have made me desperate, I want to hasten the relief, to intensify and to end the torture, as one strikes an unendurably painful hand against the trunk of a tree, regardless of everything.

There are portraits of a woman and a little girl, small amateur photographs taken against an ivy-clad wall. Along with them are letters. I take them out and try to read them. Most of it I do not understand, it is so hard to decipher and I scarcely know any French. But each word I translate pierces me like a shot in the chest;—like a stab in the chest.

My brain is taxed beyond endurance. But I realize this much, that I will never dare to write to these people as I intended. Impossible. I look at the portraits once more; they are clearly not rich people. I might send them money anonymously if I earn anything later on. I seize upon that, it is at least something to hold on to. This dead man is bound up with my life, therefore I must do everything, promise everything in order to save myself; I swear blindly that I mean to live only for his sake and his family, with wet lips I try to placate him—and deep down in me lies the hope that I may buy myself off in this way and perhaps even get out of this; it is a little stratagem: if only I am allowed to escape, then I will see to it. So I open the book and read slowly:—Gérard Duval, compositor.

With the dead man's pencil I write the address on an envelope, then swiftly thrust everything back into his tunic.

I have killed the printer, Gérard Duval. I must be a printer, I think confusedly, be a printer, printer—

By afternoon I am calmer. My fear was groundless. The name troubles me no more. The madness passes. "Comrade," I say to the dead man, but I say it calmly, "to-day you, to-morrow me. But if I come out of it, comrade, I will fight against this, that has struck us both down; from you, taken life—and from me—? Life also. I promise you, comrade. It shall never happen again."

The sun strikes low, I am stupefied with exhaustion and hunger. Yesterday is like a fog to me, there is no hope of ever getting out of this. I fall into a doze and do not at first realize that evening is approaching. The twilight comes. It seems to me to come quickly now. One hour more. If it were summer, it would be three hours more. One hour more.

Now suddenly I begin to tremble; something might happen in the interval. I think no more of the dead man, he is of no consequence to me now. With one bound the lust to live flares up again and everything that has filled my thoughts goes down before it. Now, merely to avert any ill-luck, I babble mechanically: "I will fulfill everything, fulfill everything I have promised you—" but already I know that I shall not do so.

# *Part Two*

*In some strange way the birds we kill fly on forever. Perhaps it's the broken arc, the interrupted parabola, the high zig through the alders that never quite made it to zag—all those incompletions crying out to be consummated. But something there is that keeps them airborne if only in our hearts, their wings forever roaring at the base of our trigger fingers. The partridge that puffs to the shot string this morning at the edge of some frost-crisp apple orchard in the hills of Vermont is the selfsame bird—but totally different, of course—as the very first dove we knocked down, a lifetime ago, over a Midwestern cornfield. And watched in disbelief the pale feathers spill slowly from a saffron sky. . . . Sometimes, drunk or dreaming, I see the world crisscrossed in a webwork of avian force fields, the flight paths of ghost birds winging on out as if they'd never been hit. In the end, of course, they will weave our own rough winding sheets.*

—Robert F. Jones
"EVERYTHING YOUR HEART DESIRES" (1985)

# THE PASSENGER PIGEON
## *Ectopostes migratoria,* Linn.

John James Audubon

THE PASSENGER PIGEON, or, as it is usually named in America, the Wild Pigeon, moves with extreme rapidity, propelling itself by quickly repeated flaps of the wings, which it brings more or less near to the body, according to the degree of velocity which is required. Like the Domestic Pigeon, it often flies, during the love season, in a circling manner, supporting itself with both wings angularly elevated, in which position it keeps them until it is about to alight. Now and then, during these circular flights, the tips of the primary quills of each wing are made to strike against each other, producing a smart rap, which may be heard at a distance of thirty or forty yards. Before alighting, the Wild Pigeon, like the Carolina Parrot and a few other species of birds, breaks the force of its flight by repeated flappings, as if apprehensive of receiving injury from coming too suddenly into contact with the branch or the spot of ground on which it intends to settle.

I have commenced my description of this species with the above account of its flight, because the most important facts connected with its habits relate to its migrations. These are entirely owing to the necessity of procuring food, and are not performed with the view of escaping the severity of a northern latitude, or of seeking a southern one for the purpose of breeding. They consequently do not take place at any fixed period or season of the year. Indeed, it sometimes happens that a continuance of a sufficient supply of food in one district will keep these birds absent from another for years. I know, at least, to a certainty, that in Kentucky they remained for several years constantly, and were nowhere else to be found. They all suddenly disappeared one season when the mast was exhausted, and did not return for a long period. Similar facts have been observed in other States.

Their greater power of flight enables them to survey and pass over an astonishing extent of country in a very short time. This is proved by facts well known. Thus, Pigeons have been killed in the neighborhood of New York, with their crops full of rice, which they must have collected in the fields of Georgia and Carolina, these districts being the nearest in which they could possibly have procured a supply of that kind of food. As their power of digestion is so great that they will decompose food entirely in twelve hours, they must in this case have traveled between three and four hundred miles in six hours, which shews their speed to be an average of about one mile in a minute. A velocity such as this would enable one of these birds, were it so inclined, to visit the European continent in less than three days.

This great power of flight is seconded by as great a power of vision, which enables them, as they travel at that swift rate, to inspect the country below, discover their food with facility, and thus attain the object for which their journey has been undertaken. This I have also proved to be the case, by having observed them, when passing over a sterile part of the country, or one scantily furnished with food suited to them, keep high in the air, flying with an extended front, so as to enable them to survey hundreds of acres at once. On the contrary, when the land is richly covered with food, or the trees abundantly hung with mast, they fly low, in order to discover the part most plentifully supplied.

Their body is of an elongated oval form, steered by a long well-plumed tail, and propelled by well-set wings, the muscles of which are very large and powerful for the size of the bird. When an individual is seen gliding through the woods and close to the observer, it passes like a thought, and on trying to see it again, the eye searches in vain; the bird is gone.

The multitudes of Wild Pigeons in our woods are astonishing. Indeed, after having viewed them so often, and under so many circumstances, I even now feel inclined to pause, and assure myself that what I am going to relate is fact. Yet I have seen it all, and that too in the company of persons who, like myself, were struck with amazement.

In the autumn of 1813, I left my house at Henderson, on the banks of the Ohio, on my way to Louisville. In passing over the Barrens a few miles beyond Hardensburgh, I observed the Pigeons flying from north-east to south-west, in greater numbers than I thought I had ever seen before, and feeling the inclination to count the flocks that might pass within the reach of my eye in one hour, I dismounted, seated myself on an eminence, and began to mark with my pencil, making a dot for every flock that passed. In a short time finding the task I had undertaken impracticable, as the birds poured in in countless multitudes, I rose, and counting the dots then put down, found that 163 had been made in twenty-one minutes. I traveled on, and still met more the farther I proceeded. The air was literally filled with Pigeons; the light of noonday was obscured as by an eclipse; the dung fell in spots, not unlike melting flakes of snow; and the continued buzz of wings had a tendency to lull my senses to repose.

While waiting for dinner at Young's inn at the confluence of Salt river with the Ohio, I saw, at my leisure, immense legions still going by, with a front reaching far beyond the Ohio on the west, and the beechwood forests directly on the east of me. Not a single bird alighted; for not a nut or acorn was that year to be seen in the neighborhood. They consequently flew so high, that different trials to reach them with a capital rifle proved ineffectual; nor did the reports disturb them in the least. I cannot describe to you the extreme beauty of their aerial evolutions, when a Hawk chanced to press upon the rear of the flock. At once, like a torrent, and with a noise like thunder, they rushed into a compact mass, pressing upon each other towards the center. In these almost solid masses, they darted forward in undulating and angular lines, descended and swept close to the earth with inconceivable velocity, mounted perpendicularly so as to resemble a vast column, and, when high, were seen wheeling and twisting within their continued lines, which then resembled the coils of a gigantic serpent.

Before sunset I reached Louisville, distant from Hardensburgh fifty-five miles. The Pigeons were still passing in undiminished numbers, and continued to do so for three days in succession. The people were all in arms. The banks of the Ohio were crowded with men and boys, incessantly shooting at the pilgrims, which there flew lower as they passed the river. Multitudes were thus destroyed. For a week or more, the population fed on no other flesh than that of Pigeons, and talked of nothing but Pigeons.

It is extremely interesting to see flock after flock performing exactly the same evolutions which had been traced as it were in the air by a preceding flock. Thus, should a Hawk have charged on a group at a certain spot, the angles, curves, and undulations that have been described by the birds, in their efforts to escape the dreaded talons of the plunderers, are undeviatingly followed by the next group that comes up. Should the bystander happen to witness one of these affrays, and, struck with the rapidity and elegance of the motions exhibited, feel desirous of seeing them repeated, his wishes will be gratified if he only remain in the place until the next group comes up.

As soon as the Pigeons discover a sufficiency of food to entice them to alight, they fly around in circles, reviewing the country below. During their evolutions, on such occasions, the dense mass which they form exhibits a beautiful appearance, as it changes direction, now displaying a glistening sheet of azure, when the backs of the birds come simultaneously into view, and anon, suddenly presenting a mass of rich deep purple. They then pass lower, over the woods, and for a moment are lost among the foliage, but again emerge, and are seen gliding aloft. They now alight, but the next moment, as if suddenly alarmed, they take to wing, producing by the flappings of their wings a noise like the roar of distant thunder, and sweep through the forests to see if danger is near. Hunger, however, soon brings them to the ground. When alighted, they are seen industriously throwing up the withered leaves in quest of the fallen mast. The rear ranks are continually rising, passing over the mainbody, and alighting in front, in such rapid succession, that the whole flock seems still on the wing. The quantity of ground thus swept is astonishing, and so completely has it been cleared, that the gleaner who might follow in their rear would find his labor completely lost. Whilst feeding, their avidity is at times so great that in attempting to swallow a large acorn or nut, they are seen gasping for a long while, as if in the agonies of suffocation.

On such occasions, when the woods are filled with these Pigeons, they are killed in immense numbers, although no apparent diminution ensues. About the middle of the day, after their repast is finished, they settle on the trees, to enjoy rest, and digest their food. On the ground they walk with ease, as well as on the branches, frequently jerking their beautiful tail, and moving the neck backwards and forwards in the most graceful manner. As the sun begins to sink beneath the horizon, they depart *en masse* for the roosting-place, which not unfrequently is hundreds of miles distant, as has been ascertained by persons who have kept an account of their arrivals and departures.

Let us now, kind reader, inspect their place of nightly rendezvous. One of these curious roosting-places, on the banks of the Green river in Kentucky, I repeatedly visited. It was, as is always the case, in a portion of forest where the trees are of great magnitude, and where there is little underwood. I rode through it upwards of forty miles, and, crossing it in different parts, found its average breadth to be rather more than three miles. My first view of it was about a fortnight subsequent to the period when they had made a choice of it, and I arrived there nearly two hours before sunset. Few Pigeons were then to be seen, but a great number of persons, with horses and wagons, guns and ammunition, had already established encampments on the borders. Two farmers from the vicinity of Russelville, distant more that a hundred miles, had driven upwards of three hundred hogs to be fattened on the pigeons which were to be slaughtered. Here and there, the people employed in plucking and salting what they had already procured, were seen sitting in the midst of large piles of these birds. The dung lay several inches deep, covering the whole extent of the roosting-place. Many trees two feet in diameter, I observed, were broken off at no great distance from the ground; and the branches of many of the largest and tallest had given way, as if the forest had been swept by a tornado. Every thing proved to me that the number of birds resorting to this part of the forest must be immense beyond conception. As the period of their arrival approached, their foes anxiously waited prepared to receive them. Some were furnished with iron-pots containing sulphur, other with torches of pine-knots, many with poles, and the rest with guns. The sun was lost to our view, yet not a Pigeon had arrived. Every thing was ready, and all eyes were gazing on the clear sky, which appeared in glimpses amidst the tall trees. Suddenly there burst forth a general cry of "Here they come!" The noise which they made, though yet distant, reminded me of a hard gale at sea, passing through the rigging of a close-reefed vessel. As the birds arrived and passed over me, I felt a current of air that surprised me. Thousands were soon knocked down by the pole-men. The birds continued to pour in. The fires were lighted, and a magnificent, as well as wonderful and almost terrifying, sight presented itself. The Pigeons, arriving by the thousands, alighted everywhere, one above another, until solid masses were formed on the branches all round. Here and there the perches gave way under the weight with a crash, and, falling to the ground, destroyed hundreds of the birds beneath, forcing down the dense groups with which every stick was loaded. It was a scene of uproar and confusion. I found it quite useless to speak, or even shout to those persons who were nearest to me. Even the reports of the guns were seldom heard, and I was made aware of the firing only by seeing the shooters reloading.

No one dared venture within the line of devastation. The hogs had been penned up in due time, the pickings of the dead and wounded being left for the next morning's employment. The Pigeons were constantly coming, and it was past midnight before I perceived a decrease in the number of those that arrived. The uproar continued the whole night; and as I was anxious to know to what distance the sound reached, I sent off a man, accustomed to perambulate the forest, who, returning two hours afterwards, informed me he had heard it distinctly when three miles distant from the spot. Towards the approach of day, the noise in some measure subsided: long before objects were distinguishable, the Pigeons began to move off in a direction quite different from that in which they had arrived the evening before, and at sunrise all that were able to fly had disappeared. The howlings of the wolves now reached our ears, and the foxes, lynxes, cougars, bears, raccoons, opossums and pole-cats were seen sneaking off, whilst eagles and hawks of different species, accompanied by a crowd of vultures, came to supplant them, and enjoy their share of the spoil.

It was then that the authors of all this devastation began their entry amongst the dead, the dying, and the mangled. The Pigeons were picked up and piled in heaps, until each had as many as he could possibly dispose of, when the hogs were let loose to feed on the remainder.

Persons unacquainted with these birds might naturally conclude that such dreadful havoc would soon put an end to the species. But I have satisfied myself, by long observation, that nothing but the gradual diminution of the forest can accomplish their decrease, as they not unfrequently quadruple their numbers yearly, and always at least double it.

# Thinking Like a Mountain

Aldo Leopold

A DEEP CHESTY bawl echoes from rimrock to rimrock, rolls down the mountain, and fades into the far blackness of the night. It is an outburst of wild defiant sorrow, and of contempt for all the adversities of the world.

Every living thing (and perhaps many a dead one as well) pays heed to that call. To the deer it is a reminder of the way of all flesh, to the pine a forecast of midnight scuffles and of blood upon the snow, to the coyote a promise of gleanings to come, to the cowman a thread of red ink at the bank, to the hunter a challenge of fang against bullet. Yet behind these obvious and immediate hopes and fears there lies a deeper meaning, known only to the mountain itself. Only the mountain has lived long enough to listen objectively to the howl of a wolf.

Those unable to decipher the hidden meaning know nevertheless that it is there, for it is felt in all wolf country, and distinguishes that country from all other land. It tingles in the spine of all who hear wolves by night, or who scan their tracks by day. Even without sight or sound of wolf, it is implicit in a hundred small events: the midnight whinny of a pack horse, the rattle of rolling rocks, the bound of a fleeing deer, the way shadows lie under the spruces. Only the ineducable tyro can fail to sense the presence or absence of wolves, or the fact that mountains have a secret opinion about them.

My own conviction on this score dates from the day I saw a wolf die. We were eating lunch on a high rimrock, at the foot of which a turbulent river elbowed its way. We saw what we thought was a doe fording the torrent, her breast awash in white water. When she climbed the bank toward us and shook out her tail, we realized our error: it was a wolf. A half-dozen others, evidently grown pups, sprang from the willows and all joined in a welcoming mêlée of wagging tails and playful maulings. What was literally a pile of wolves writhed and tumbled in the center of an open flat at the foot of our rimrock.

In those days we had never heard of passing up a chance to kill a wolf. In a second we were pumping lead into the pack, but with more excitement than accuracy: how to aim a steep downhill shot is always confusing. When our rifles were empty, the old wolf was down, and a pup was dragging a leg into impassable slide-rocks.

We reached the old wolf in time to watch a fierce green fire dying in her eyes. I realized then, and have known ever since, that there was something new to me in those eyes—something known only to her and to the mountain. I was young then, and full of trigger-itch; I thought that because fewer wolves meant more deer, that no wolves would mean hunters' paradise. But after seeing the green fire die, I sensed that neither the wolf nor the mountain agreed with such a view.

Since then I have lived to see state after state extirpate its wolves. I have watched the face of many a newly wolfless mountain, and seen the south-facing slopes wrinkle with a maze of new deer trails. I have seen every edible bush and seedling browsed, first to anemic desuetude, and then to death. I have seen every edible tree defoliated to the height of a saddle horn. Such a mountain looks as if someone had given God a new pruning shears, and forbidden Him all other exercise. In the end the starved bones of the hoped-for deer herd, dead of its own too-much, bleach with the bones of the dead sage, or molder under the high-lined junipers.

I now suspect that just as a deer herd lives in mortal fear of its wolves, so does a mountain live in mortal fear of its deer. And perhaps with better cause, for while a buck pulled down by wolves can be replaced in two or three years, a range pulled down by too many deer may fail of replacement in as many decades.

So also with cows. The cowman who cleans his range of wolves does not realize that he is taking over the wolf's job of trimming the herd to fit the range. He has not learned to think like a mountain. Hence we have dustbowls, and rivers washing the future into the sea.

# Part Three

*To tell the truth, I wish I could put them back in the trees the way they were
this morning.*

—Fred Bucklin, a Massachusetts market hunter
who killed as many as 350 grouse and woodcock
a day in the 1890s, to his daughter
after a meager all-day hunt (two grouse,
two woodcock) in the 1920s.
Quoted in Frank Woolner's
GROUSE AND GROUSE HUNTING (1970).

# A FEW THOUGHTS ON ADAM'S CURSE

## Dan Gerber

As THE SUN begins to burn through the morning fog my eye is drawn to a curious movement in the grass. Two quail, in their odd, pizzicato gait, scurry past my window, and I see them simultaneously as divine fellow creatures and succulent roasted delights. I won't kill these lovely neighbors to put them on my plate—those days are over for me—though I'd be delighted to join any one of my still predatory friends to savor them with a little foie gras, garlic potatoes, and a bottle of Di Bruno Sangiovese. I know that this imagined feast to which I seek an invitation, will be a sacrament, and that my friends will not have taken these lives without an awareness of their own mortality and also, without a touch of regret.

*Killing too is a form of our ancient wandering affliction,* to borrow from Rilke, a form of Adam's curse, as is the language through which I must labor to discover what I am trying to say here. The birthright of Esau, the hunter, has been usurped by Jacob, the herdsman, yet both would kill to court favor with their father.

There is a wonderful passage in *The Upanishads:*
"Oh wonderful, oh wonderful, oh wonderful,
I am food, I am food, I am food,
I am an eater of food. I am an eater of food. I am an eater of food."

Joseph Campbell suggests that clinging to yourself and not letting yourself become food is the primary, life-denying act that runs counter to the great mystery experience of thanking the animal one is about to eat for haven given itself. For we realize that in the realm of *real* time, it is always ourselves we are eating.

I wonder how many hunters today, how many so-called sportsmen, carry this kind of awareness about what they are doing, let alone how many kill a being—a lion, a wolf, or a trophy bull—they have no intention of eating? How many kill with empathy for the animal? How many see themselves as food? We are life feeding on life, the most fundamental fact of our existence, and if we are not aware of and grateful to the various spirits who give up their lives to sustain us, mere existence, not life, is our portion. *And whoever walks a furlong without sympathy*—Whitman warns us—*walks to his own funeral dressed in his shroud.*

On a sultry afternoon in Key West almost twenty-five years ago, Truman Capote told me about all the mass murderers he has interviewed. He told me that the one thing they all had in common was that they broke into uncontrollable laughter when they told him, in detail, about the actual acts of killing they had performed. Tears streamed down their cheeks as they tried to contain themselves to finish their stories. And, without exception, they apologized to him, saying, "I'm sorry. I know this isn't funny to you, but it was funny to me when I did it."

This is something we learned—or should never have forgotten—reading *Macbeth,* that what distinguishes the cold-blooded killer is his, or her, lack of imagination, his utter lack of empathy, that he is able to kill without ever imagining himself on the receiving end, that he is incapable of imagining himself as a victim.

My father was passionate about bird hunting, and so I grew up as a hunter. I have cherished memories of the sonar-like conversations by which we would keep track of other's whereabouts as we stalked pheasants through a field of tall corn and of time spent together—time we probably wouldn't have otherwise shared—as the predawn mist rose from the water surrounding our duck blind while we shivered indistinguishably through the chill and our anticipation of the first pass of canvasbacks.

And later, in my teens, I'd often get up at 4:00 a.m. on a late fall morning and paddle through the marsh with my friend, Bob VandenBerg, to spend an hour or two before Mr. Cooper's economics class watching over our decoys while we broke football training rules with our furtive pack of Mapleton cigarettes. And I have other less fond memories, of mornings when the ducks never appeared and we exorcised our boredom and our idle lust blasting inedible coots simply because they were within range. Their blood darkened the bilge of our boat and their limp bodies condemned me like the albatross of *The Ancient Mariner*, long after we pitched them into the cattails as we paddled home.

Though I miss the camaraderie of upland hunting, the intricate work with the dogs, and the satisfaction of weariness and well earned appetite at the end of a long day in the field, I never hunted without feeling a little bit conflicted, never enjoyed it without a mild accompanying sense of dread and a touch of regret each time the rules of the game required me to take a life. There was always that sobering moment. Maybe I'm a more blatant hypocrite now. Maybe we all are to some degree, but there finally came that day when I held the warm, still-fluttering body of a downed woodcock in my hand and saw for a moment my own eye reflected in his before I put his lights out against the butt of my gun. And I knew then that I didn't want to do this anymore. Maybe I'd gotten soft. Maybe it was a heightened sense of my own mortality. Maybe age. Maybe all of these.

Often, when we look very closely at any given realm of life what we see is a world of terror as in the ultimate dominion of decay, the terror of the pewit about to be impaled by the merlin, of whatever creature my fly may at the moment be imitating as it is devoured by the trout, and of the trout itself, being bullied inevitably in its struggle toward the shore to be beheaded and stripped of its meat. And yet when we step back to a more encompassing window, even now to see the earth itself from the point of view of the moon, we see all these minute tyrannies as the finely woven threads of a complete and flourishing fabric. What ruthless horde of microbes may, at this moment, be scourging the plains of my hand?

I'm still a meat eater, and I am still a flyfisher. Last night I killed a two-pound rainbow trout for my supper and savored it both as a delicacy and as a sacrament of the interdependent nature of our existence, while at the same time having serious second thoughts even about the undeniable pain and distress I cause the trout or tarpon I catch and release for my pleasure.

Recently, my oldest and dearest friend, a man who keeps October sacrosanct and will brook no interference whatsoever with grouse season, confessed that he's been having second thoughts. "Hunting is so final," he mused, "so Wagnerian, while fishing seems to have an almost Mozartian lightness about it. In fishing, at least, most of the time, you have the option of returning the fish to its life. There is no catch-and-release hunting."

Just now I lay down my pen to swat a yellow jacket my dog was worrying against the window glass. I did it to prevent my dog from getting stung and to protect myself as well. The minor threat is past, and the yellow jacket lies curled in death on the windowsill. What the answer is, I don't know. With Rilke, I'm resolved to live the questions.

From

# FARMER

## Jim Harrison

JOSEPH HAD ALWAYS spent a great deal of time trying to think analytically about his main preoccupations, which were fishing and hunting. As the years passed he found he had less and less interest in the mere act of acquiring fish and game. For instance he no longer shot ducks. Not only were they easy but they were simply too fascinating to watch on the beaver pond way back in the center of the state tract. If you spent a long time on your stalk you could get close enough to watch them for hours. It was much more difficult with Canada geese, surely the wariest of all birds. But the ducks, most commonly mallards, mergansers, teal, or blue bills, would complacently swim and speak their odd language. Joseph experimented in alarming them. Sometimes it required only an upraised hand wagging from cover but if they were feeding avidly enough you could stand and shout before they would flush. The geese always kept several scouts on the periphery of their feeding area to alert them to any danger.

On the Sunday morning after his meeting with Catherine he sat by the pond for a couple of hours watching the birds, and the peacefulness of sitting so long amid this beauty drew him to questions that seem essential to everyone. An idea that fixed him to one spot was that life was a death dance and that he had quickly passed through the spring and summer of his life and was halfway through the fall. He had to do a better job on the fall because everyone on earth knew what the winter was like. The ocean creatures he read of illustrated the point so bleakly. To devour and be devoured. But their sure instincts kept them alive as long as possible, as did those of the wild ducks before him, or the geese. Even the brook trout, the simplest of the trout family, were mindful of the waterbirds, the kingfisher and heron, that fed on them.

One afternoon he had been lucky enough to see a Cooper's hawk swoop down through the trees and kill a blue-winged teal. The other ducks escaped in a wild flock circling the pond twice while the Cooper's hawk stood shrouding its prey with its wings. Joseph watched it feed on the teal's breast then fly off to a large dead oak to preen. It was far too spectacular to be disturbing. *Once in town he had seen a car turn a corner and strike a lady pedestrian. He could still see the shocked, twisted look on her face.* A couple of hours later a few ducks circled the pond hesitantly. Soon they had all returned to their feeding.

For Joseph there were presentiments of the troubles to come even before he had begun his affair with Catherine. He had left half the apples unpicked and for the first time didn't want any school children in the orchard. What little heart he had left for teaching was gone before the end of September; he met each morning feeling a certain dread mixed with lassitude. He spent far less time in the tavern playing cards and far more time reading about distant places. All of the strictures, habits, the rules of order for both work and pleasure seemed to be rending at even the strong points.

October grouse season had always been the high point of his sporting year along with late May and early June and the heavy mayfly hatches of trout fishing. He would rush home from school leaving Rosealee to lock up, change his clothes, and hunt with old Dr. Evans until the fall light disappeared. He would hunt all day Saturday after the chores were done and on Sunday from dawn to dark. But this year the doctor had decided to give up hunting—his legs would no longer take the strenuous walking. The doctor had presented Joseph with his fine Parker shotgun in August: Joseph had coveted the expensive gun for years, the beautifully grained whorl of its walnut stock and the fine engraving of a pointing dog along the breech. But when the season began this time everything conspired against him: the weather was cold and wet, making his leg ache more than ordinary, then the weather changed into an over-warm and humid Indian summer, and grouse were near the bottom of their seven-year population cycle, though woodcock were plentiful.

It was a male woodcock that pinpointed a certain loss of nerve. After sunup one Sunday he walked along the west fence border of the farm, back toward the corner where the creek and swamp joined the state property. It was a splendid morning with white frost on the pasture; clear, cold, with the ferns finally dead and the walking easy. He approached a blackberry swale and for a moment pretended he was gesturing his old bird dog, a Springer spaniel, into the blackberries to flush the birds. But the dog was long dead. Joseph stood there and stared at a weak sun climbing over the swamp. A woodcock flushed at his feet toward the sun and he lost it for a moment but then it dipped below the treetop and he dropped the bird easily. He walked over and picked up the bird but it fluttered in the tall canary grass, still alive. He caught it and began to wring its neck but the woodcock's large brown eyes followed his movements. He turned the bird around but the bird twisted its neck toward Joseph still staring at him with a glint of the morning sun shining off its retinas. Joseph closed his own eyes and snapped its spine near the neck. He shoved the bird into the game bag in his vest but he was trembling.

Joseph sat down on a pile of old fence posts and thought about the woodcock. How could he become so nervous after thirty years of hunting? He had never looked into a bird's eyes before and it had at least temporarily unnerved him. He tried to ignore how nearly human the eyes looked, but he couldn't rid his mind totally of the idea: eyes are what we hold most in common in terms of similarity to other beasts. He always cringed when he hooked a fish in the eye. When they slaughtered both cattle and pigs the eyes stayed open in death. But it was more than that; the woodcock was warm, palpable, it quivered, and its eyes did not blink under his gaze.

By mid-morning he had bagged two grouse but had missed several woodcock. He sat on a stump near the creek and slowly ate his sandwich, wondering if he had missed the woodcock on purpose. They were normally far easier to shoot than grouse. Did it mean, too, that one more pleasure was to be denied him on his already severely atrophied list of enthusiasms? He had sensed that the energies that fed his interests had somehow diminished but he believed these energies would recover and persist. Only it wasn't happening and the near frenzy that had occurred with Catherine the week before was the first "new" thing to enter his life in a long time. Sitting there on the stump with the sun warming his back and drying the dew from his pant cuffs he felt bovine, immovable; he numbered his passions: he had loved Rosealee for thirty years, he had hunted and fished for thirty-five years and worked hard on the farm nearly that long, almost assuming manhood at eight when he learned to walk again, and he had taught twenty-three years though that was more menial habit than passion. You had to count reading about subjects that were least in touch with his own life. But these simple things had truly filled his life and he knew them so intimately that an edge of panic entered him on considering that they might simply blow away like clouds. He could not comprehend it; the earth looked the same and this October day was not unlike a hundred other October days. He looked at the odd way his heels wore off his boots because of his walk. Even the stump was a familiar chair. Should he blame the woodcock's eyes or Catherine's body or his own fatuous brain for losing control? He looked at the fence which was in disrepair and again felt guilty about the apples. How many blankets had his mother quilted for his marriage to Rosealee? Why did he drink more and read less, and why did his favorite books bore him? He knew in some oblique way that he was no longer his father's son. He despaired that forty-three was too late for new conclusions, but he knew this was a lie. One of the doctor's favorite speeches when he was drunk was how grief made people lazy, torpid. Joseph wanted to believe that that was only the doctor's profession, that the doctor was vaguely buggy from seeing so much death. But it was too easy to remember the necessary deaths of so many of the farm animals he had been close to, how even the execution of an awful, cantankerous rooster had touched him.

On the way back to the house he shot another grouse. The grouse flushed toward him and flew low over some sumac. He made a difficult shot and that warmed him somewhat. Now there was enough for dinner. Rosealee was coming for dinner and he looked forward to their comforting though pointless conversations on whether he should begin farming full-time next year. They had accumulated a stack of equipment catalogs but the catalogs were far less interesting to Joseph than books on the ocean. He was startled by an urge to throw the woodcock into the weeds in order not to have to look at it again. But he hadn't fallen apart that much. To waste game was the ultimate crime: he despised hunters who shot crows for what they called "sport" or under the assumption that crows fed on duck eggs. Crows stayed on the farm year round and after decades of studying their habits Joseph believed the crow to be the sole bird with any wit.

The unnerving incident followed him around throughout the season and the more he tried to erase the image of the woodcock the more insistent its presence became. He looked into the eyes of a dead grouse and felt nothing. The doctor thought of grouse as small gray chickens that flushed wildly and flew at fifty miles an hour. But they were without much character; if a chicken fed on wintergreen, chokecherries, wild grape, it would taste as good as a grouse. Grouse were splendid dinners wandering around in the forest waiting to be gathered and eaten. Now Joseph removed woodcock from this food category and allowed them to join the highest strata, that of the owls and hawks, the raptors, harriers, the *Falconiformes*. This made hunting much more difficult and his average bag dropped to the level he owned as a neophyte; he could no longer "point shoot" on instinct at the flush but had to wait an extra split second to make sure it was the gray flush of a grouse rather than the golden brown of the woodcock. His mother no longer asked him, how many, Yoey? when he came in from the hunting, noticing the irritation of his voice when he replied.

# A QUESTION OF BLESSINGS

## Robert F. Jones

ON A QUIET evening last spring I went out behind the house at dusk, into our fifteen-acre meadow, to catch the Woodcock Sonata. The time was 8:35 p.m., the evening windless and mild; the last light of day was fading to blue velvet. All was silence.

But then, right on schedule, came the sound I'd been waiting to hear: the faint, nasal, rasping *peent* of a woodcock announcing the sky dance which constitutes his courtship. The buzzing call was infrequent, about once every ten or twenty seconds, and lasted for three or four minutes overall. His overture complete, the bird launched himself on twittering wings straight upwards into the evening. Up, up he spiraled, twittering all the way—one hundred feet, two hundred, three—out of the deepening darkness and into the last of the light. Then he dive-bombed the earth in a long zigzag glide, burbling his flight-song, a series of wild, liquid chirps . . .

The woodcock landed not far from his takeoff point, and soon the peenting began again. For the next half hour the airborne

Romeo and I had the evening to ourselves. Eventually, I knew, these serenades would attract a female of the species to the edge of the meadow. After mating, while Romeo flew off in search of another conquest, his erstwhile Juliet would scratch a crude nest in the field, sometimes close to a scraggly shrub or two but more often right out in the open. A woodcock nest is nothing fancy, a mere scrape edged with a low berm of twigs and grasses. In it she'll lay four buff-colored eggs, mottled a rusty brown, that look too large for such a small bird. She incubates the eggs for about three weeks. The hatchlings can follow the hen on foot and actually feed themselves only a day or two after hatching, probing the mucky ground for worms just like Mommy. In four weeks they are full grown and flying, and by eight weeks they're entirely on their own.

Yet during the brief time the young spend with their mother, she attends them much more carefully than many other female birds, covering her chicks from rain and snow, protecting them with her subtle camouflage from wandering predators. Indeed, the nineteenth- and early-twentieth-century literature on the woodcock, admittedly anecdotal, reports many cases of mother woodcock actually *carrying* their young away from danger, and on the wing at that.

Edwyn Sandys, an expatriate English hunter-naturalist whose book *Upland Game Birds* (Macmillan, 1902) is one of my most prized possessions, writes:

> I have good reason to believe that I have seen one carried off. The nest in question was on a bit of level ground amid tall trees. The sole suggestion of cover was a lot of flattened leaves that lay as the snow had left them. Perhaps ten yards away was an old rail fence about waist-high, and on the farther side of it was a clump of tall saplings. A man coming out of the wood told me he had just flushed a woodcock and had seen her brood, recently hatched, and pointed out where they were. I went in to investigate, and located one young bird crouched on the leaves. It ran a few steps and

*again crouched, evidently not yet strong enough for any sustained effort. I went off, and hid behind a stump, to await developments. From this shelter the young bird was visible and it made no attempt to move. Presently the old one came fluttering back, alighted near the youngster, and walked to it. In a few moments she rose and flew low and heavily, merely clearing the fence, and dropping perhaps ten yards within the thicket. Her legs appeared to be half-bent, and so far as I could determine the youngster was held between them. Something about her appearance reminded me of a thing often seen—a shrike carrying off a small bird. I carefully marked her down, then glanced toward where the youngster had been. It was no longer there; and a few moments later it, or its mate, was found exactly where the mother had gone down. . . . These details are dwelt on because many writers have disputed the carrying of the young. My impression is that the bird had removed the other children before I got to the place. They certainly were not beside the one, but the search for them was brief, owing to the fact that there was a nasty possibility of stepping on them.*

An odd bird indeed is my friend *Philohela minor.* Oh yes, I know the taxonomists recently changed his name to the uneuphonious *Scolopax minor,* but I'm an old curmudgeon now and I'm damned if I'll honor the alteration. Known colloquially as timberdoodle, bog-sucker, even mudbat, the woodcock is the strangest, dearest bird I know, and I won't change his name on a whim of mere science.

Consider this odd-ball object of my affections:

A woodcock's brain, for some reason, is mounted upside down.

Its ears are located forward of its nostrils.

Its huge, dark, bulging eyes, which sit high toward the back of a tiny, pinched-in head, can scan a full 360 degrees, the better to elude its enemies—which are legion. Were our eyes as large in proportion, they'd each be the size of a grapefruit.

Add to this a disproportionately long bill—2½ inches in the male, 3 in the female—a bill which is flexible at the tip and as sensitive as a pair of human fingers, allowing the woodcock to grasp its favorite food source, earthworms, more deftly than your fingers can retrieve an errant strand of spaghetti on a slippery plate; a virtually nonexistent tail; a pair of dainty, coral-pink feet; wings that look too broad and long for a bird that weighs only a little more than six ounces—wings more suitable to a barn owl or a small hawk—and a wondrous, dodgy, batlike agility in flight, and you have an unlikely object for human affection.

The woodcock and his larger mate (females of the species weigh eight ounces or more) can cover two or three hundred miles a night during their migrations, but usually they fly alone, or with a few close friends—leisurely spring or fall flights of no more than twenty to fifty miles each, depending on the weather.

A woodcock can eat twice its weight in worms each day in preparation for these seasonal flights.

The animals that like to eat *him,* along with his wife and his progeny (either eggs or chicks) include owls, hawks, crows, ravens, shrikes, bobcats, coyotes, foxes, dogs, housecats, snakes, raccoons, skunks, weasels, and the odd human hunter. Woodcock are not popular prey among bird hunters, but the hunting pressure on them is certainly increasing, particularly in the South, where wild quail populations—the traditional bird of choice among rural Southerners—have nearly ceased to exist. Pen-raised, planted quail are abundant on expensive plantations, to be sure, but the working-class Dixie bird hunter can't afford to hunt them and so the wild woodcock has slowly become more important to these blue collar gunners. Yet the woodcock's worst enemies are the land developer and those misguided activists who oppose clear-cutting.

Though the woodcock is not yet in danger of extinction—nearly two million birds a year are bagged legally by hunters over the woodcock's migratory range, east of the Mississippi from southern Canada to the Louisiana bamboo thickets hard by the Gulf of

Mexico—they've been declining over the past dozen years or more at an annual rate of three percent. This figure is arrived at by admittedly sketchy counts made at the woodcock's singing grounds during the spring mating season, yet no ornithologist has any idea of the total number of woodcock in North America. That fact alone renders the decline suspect, but I have no doubt from my own experience in the field that it is indeed occurring. The main reason for this is loss of habitat. To thrive, woodcock need young successional forests dotted with brushy, overgrowing meadows, but we are allowing our woodlands to get too damned old—not just in Vermont, but throughout the Northeast.

The boom time for woodcock in this country occurred from the turn of the century through the Great Depression of the 1930s. During those years family farms were abandoned at an ever increasing rate as the nation turned more and more to city life. As a result, in the emptying countryside, vast patches of cleared pasture slowly returned to woodland: thick stands of sprouting aspen clouded the once-bald New England hills, and mucky, worm-rich alder brakes clotted the brooks and burns and bottomland that drained them: Timberdoodle Heaven.

By the 1960s this process was already reversing itself. Aspen had matured to pole timber and was being edged out by invading hardwoods like ash, oak, swamp maple and beech. Alders had aged past the stage where woodcock could profit from them. People fed up with life in the tumultuous cities of the northeast and their stultifying suburbs were moving into the countryside of rural, interior New England, where land was still cheap and building costs not yet excessive. Inevitably the sites these people chose for their new homes were the very places where ruffed grouse and woodcock had found their best living: wooded hilltops with brooks running nearby. The malling of America also contributed its bit to the decline of grouse and woodcock habitat: since the cheapest land was boggy or swampy, developers had only to drain it to throw up a new shopping center. And it was on the edges of those very bogs and swamps that woodcock had found their happiest worm-hunting ground. Worse still, the former city folks brought with them fallacious attitudes regarding woodland and wildlife. Clear-cutting, which could have brought back the successional stages of woodland recovery so necessary to continued woodcock populations, was and remains anathema to most ex-urbanites. Even selective logging, which does nothing to improve game habitat, is frowned upon, though it's often grudgingly accepted by city types to improve the "landscaping" of their acreage.

The only new growth that's benefited from this urbanite invasion in my neck of the woods is the Vermont State Flower, with its colorful orange and black blossoms gracing every quiet backwoods road and brook and hillside clear up to the Canadian border: *Postatus signatorus* (the Posted Sign).

Soon, though, if habitat continues to decline the way it's going, such warnings will no longer be necessary. There'll be nothing left to protect but squirrels and owls. And one day not far into the future, if human population continues to grow and sprawl the way it has, they too will be gone.

For a number of years now I've been caught up in an agonizing internal debate: Should I or should I not swear off killing woodcock? No game bird has given me more pleasure in the course of my fifty year hunting career than this plump, pint-sized, russet-clad, long-billed, bug-eyed solitary of the uplands. But as Jorrocks, the rough-and-ready fox hunter who graced the works of the English sporting writer Surtees, often said of wily Reynard and his kin, "I loves 'em, I loves 'em, I loves 'em . . . and I loves to kill 'em." When it comes to woodcock, I second that emotion.

I love to walk the autumn woods behind my dogs in search of these birds. I love it when the dog makes game and noses into a thick patch of cover, his whole demeanor changed, intense now, more than intense—vibrant. Nostrils wide, eyes gleaming, tail erect, he scans the thorny whips and red and brown leaf–blanketed undergrowth. It's almost impossible to see an unmoving woodcock against the forest floor. They hold tighter than any other game bird, sometimes not flushing until a dog's jaws, or a hunter's boot, are only inches from where they crouch. I love the unexpectedness of the flush—even when I know it's coming, the flurried, thunderclap whistle of blurring wings still delights and surprises me. You never know which way the bird will fly. I've had woodcock launch themselves directly at my face, then reverse direction in a wingbeat to line out through a maze of head-high interlaced branches that you wouldn't think would permit the passage of a sparrow. The adrenalin rush is instant, intense, and the neophyte hunter's instinct is to mount his shotgun and fire immediately, like a quick-draw artist in a Western gunfight. But that is sheer folly. The shot pattern is still too tight at close range to allow much chance of a hit, and even if you did center the bird at that short distance, five or ten yards, the still-clotted shot would tear it to bits, leaving only a mangled gobbet of bloody meat and feathers with a wing and perhaps the long-billed head still attached. You kill woodcock to eat them, and to waste even one in the course of a season is to me a culinary mortal sin.

You must wait until the bird is fifteen or twenty yards out before firing. By that time, it is dodging through the branches as twistily as a mourning dove, and gets harder to hit with each thrust of its wings. To connect on a long shot is a blessing.

Or is it? The more I've learned about woodcock and their ways over the years, the more I've grown to love them. Every thinking hunter feels a spasm of regret when he's killed what he came for, and perhaps the bird hunter feels it longer and more deeply than most. I love to walk the woods for these birds, I love the dog work, I take pride in my knowledge of cover and my skill with a shotgun, and God knows I love to eat woodcock. But can all of this make up for having snuffed out the life of a bird I truly love?

I can argue to myself that my love of hunting grows from an instinct, a million years of human evolution as a hunting animal. But I know that that's begging the issue. I no longer feel any desire to hunt big game—deer, elk, moose and the like—though I did when I was younger. I've never had any desire to hunt bears or mountain lions. So why do I still hunt birds?

There's a truism among hunters that the older we get, the less we feel like killing. That spasm of regret the young hunter feels at taking a game animal's life becomes, with age, first a nagging repugnance, and then finally an outright revulsion. It certainly seems to be true. A dear friend of mine, a former game warden in East Africa who killed hundreds of elephants and buffalo in the course of his duties as a game control officer, and who later became one of the most successful safari hunters in Africa, now tells me that he regrets every animal he ever killed. He gets tears in his eyes when he speaks of them. The popular explanation for this, of course, is that the closer we get to death, the more abhorrent to us becomes the death of any other creature. I think it's more complicated than that, though. No clear-thinking man or woman today still believes that some Old Testament God created "lesser animals" for the exclusive pleasure and use of humankind. We've ceased to recognize a clear-cut dichotomy between humans and other animals. We know now that we too are animals, and not necessarily the only ones with self-awareness.

I'm not arguing that a creature as different from us as a six-ounce, pea-brained woodcock has a "soul." But woodcock do have a distinctive, unique essence, a collection of traits and modes of behavior, that I find charming—no, downright loveable. And though I also love to pursue them, flush them, shoot at them, cook them and eat them, I love that essence more.

So here is my pledge to *Philohela minor* and all his kind: I vow that beginning this season—the first of a new millennium—I will no longer raise my gun at you, no matter how tough or tempting the shot. Grouse, quail and pheasants, yes, doves, ducks and geese, of course. Maybe even the odd starling or barn pigeon.

But woodcock, nevermore.

Of course, whether I can keep that promise on every flush remains to be seen. In the heat of action, men are likely to forget their best resolves and follow their instincts. And then again, even if I *can* control my trigger finger, maybe my dogs won't let me.

Post Script (October 2000):

Now on to a confession I'd rather not make. On my third day afield during last fall's grouse and woodcock season, I hunted my friend Ed Carmel's covert. So far I had kept my vow. Not a single woodcock had fallen to my gun. But it was not a true test of steadfastness, because on the two previous days my dogs hadn't flushed any. Still, I knew they would on Ed's land. That 65-acre parcel of sidehill alders, spring seeps, blackberry brambles, overgrown meadows, and abandoned but still productive apple trees, always produces a bumper crop of both woodcock and grouse. It was an ideal day, sunny but crisp, not too hot for my aging Labrador Jake to work at full vigor. He knows that covert like the bottom of his food bowl, and sure enough, on his first pass through a favorite patch of briers and saplings, two woodcock got up. My instincts, honed over more than half a century of upland shooting, took charge and I found myself swinging fast on an easy left-to-right passing shot, well within killing range. The instant before I hit the trigger, my willpower clicked in. I checked the swing and let the bird fly off unscathed.

It felt odd. Even as my sanctimonious superego was preening itself on adherence to my promise, something in my guts, or maybe my nerve ends, said this was all wrong. The hunter in my heart felt cheated. "Be a man," I told him silently, "a promise is a promise. Don't be greedy."

My host Ed Carmel, who doesn't hunt but loves to follow me and the dogs while we do, said he'd seen a grouse cross one of the trails he brushhogs through the covert each fall. The bird had crossed less than an hour earlier. We ambled on down the trail in that direction. Soon Jake's nose located the grouse in question and I saw it hop up into a small, leafless apple tree. Young birds will do that. Of course I wouldn't shoot it standing there motionless, but even when I yelled at it to fly, waved a free arm at it, and stamped the ground like a petulant teenager, it stayed put. I walked up, hoping to make it fly for a fair shot. The closer I came, the more clearly I could see that it was a young bird, a hen, not yet fully grown. We'd had a rainy spring and summer, and I suspect the grouse had a second hatch as they often do when their first eggs and chicks are killed off by wet, cold weather.

She was a beautiful little bird on a beautiful Sunday afternoon, the sunlight illuminating her eye like sparkling amber as she stared down at me. Jake and my Jack Russell, Roz, were zooming around the apple tree where she perched, their noses to the ground—but still she wouldn't fly. I came up to within five feet of her, could have batted her with the muzzle of the gun if I'd reached far and fast enough. "Fly, bird, fly!" I yelled again. But it was no go.

"God, she's beautiful," Ed said beside me now. "I've never seen one this close before, not unless you'd killed it."

"I can't kill her," I said, "not having looked in her eye, even if she flies like a comet." I broke the gun and dangled it over my forearm. Then Jake, following our eyes, looked up and spotted her. Seeing the dog almost eyeball to eyeball, the grouse finally flushed. Rather than ducking immediately around and behind the tree trunk and winging on out like a corkscrew, as most treed grouse will, she flew straight down the trail, never varying her flight path an inch to either side. The easiest straightaway shot one could ever hope for, a lead-pipe cinch, a dead cert. But we watched her disappear, unshot at, and she took our blessings with her.

Again the hunter within protested, but not quite as loud as before. He had other plans . . .

"There'll be another bird," I said, both to Ed and to my inner self. We started back up the trail, then headed into thick brush along a stone wall, with fragrant apples rotting underfoot. Now Roz got into the act. She darted ahead into a patch of brush and I heard a bird flush. It was the distinctive piping whirr of woodcock wings. The bird came out in a gray-brown long-winged long-billed blur.

Before I could even think, my gun was up, swinging, swinging through, and then going bang, and the woodcock tumbled, thumping dead on the ground among the rotting apples.

I picked up her up, warm and soft in my hand, blood bubbling from her long slender bill.

My vow had been broken, as I feared it might.

"In the heat of action, men are likely to forget their best resolves and follow their instincts. . . ."

I killed no more woodcock that day. I had tried to live with a vow I suspected I could never keep. I'll try again to live up to it as the seasons progress, but I'll lapse from time to time, I'm sure. The hunter in my heart will have his way.

# *Part Four*

*I think they were made to shoot because if they were not why did they give them that whirr of wings that moves you suddenly more than any love of country? Why did they make them all so good to eat and why did they make the ones with silent flight like woodcock, snipe, and lesser bustard, better even than the rest? Why does the curlew have that voice, and who thought up the plover's call, which takes the place of noise of wings, to give us that catharsis wing shooting has given to men since they stopped flying hawks and took to fowling pieces? I think that they were made to shoot and some of us were made to shoot them and if that is not so well, never say we did not tell you that we liked it.*

—Ernest Hemingway
"REMEMBERING SHOOTING-FLYING:
A KEY WEST LETTER" (1935)

From

# ANNA KARENINA

Leo Tolstoy

WAKING AT DAYBREAK Levin tried to rouse his companions. Vasenka was lying face downwards, one stockinged leg outstretched, and sleeping so soundly that he could not wake him. Oblonsky sleepily declined to budge so early. Even Laska, who had slept curled round in the hay, got up reluctantly, and lazily stretched and settled one hind leg and then the other. Levin put on his boots and stockings, took his gun, cautiously opened the creaking door of the barn, and went out into the open air. The coachmen were asleep beside the vehicles; the horses were dozing. Only one was lazily eating oats, scattering and blowing them about in the trough. The outside world was still gray.

"Why are you up so early, my dear?" the old woman of the hut asked from the doorway, addressing him in a friendly tone as a good acquaintance of long standing.

"I'm off shooting, Granny. Can I get to the marsh this way?"

"Straight along at the back; past our threshing-floors, my dear, and then by the hemp-patches. You'll find the footpath."

Treading carefully with her bare, sunburnt feet, the old woman conducted him to the threshing-floor and moved back the fence for him.

"Go straight on and you'll come upon the marsh. Our lads took the horses that way last night."

Laska bounded gaily ahead along the footpath. Levin followed with a light, brisk step, continually glancing up at the sky. He was anxious to get to the marsh before sunrise. But the sun would not wait. The moon, which had been bright when he first came out, now only gleamed like quicksilver. The pink flush of dawn, which one could not help seeing before, now had to be sought to be discerned at all. What had been vague smudges in the distant countryside were now quite distinct. They were shocks of rye. The dew, not visible till the sun was up, on the tall fragrant hemp which had already shed its pollen, drenched Levin's legs and his blouse even above the belt. In the translucent stillness of the morning the minutest sounds were audible. A bee flew past Levin's ear like the *whizz* of a bullet. He looked close, and saw another, and then a third. They all came from behind the wattle-fence of an apiary, and disappeared over the hemp-field in the direction of the marsh. The path led straight to the marsh, which was recognizable by the vapors rising from it, thicker in one place and thinner in another, so that the reeds and willow-bushes swayed like little islands in the mist. At the edge of the marsh by the road the peasant boys and men, who had pastured their horses in the night, were lying under their coats, having fallen asleep at daybreak. Near by three hobbled horses were moving about, one of them clattering its chain. Laska trotted beside her master, beseeching to be allowed to run forward, and looking around. Passing the sleeping peasants and reaching the first bog, Levin examined his percussion caps and let the dog go. One of the horses, a sleek, chestnut three-year-old, shied at the sight of Laska, switched its tail and snorted. The other horses were also startled, and splashed through the water with their hobbled feet, making a sucking sound as they drew their hooves out of the thick, clayey mud and began floundering their way out of the marsh. Laska stopped, looking derisively at the horses and inquiringly at Levin. Levin patted her, and gave a whistle to tell her she might begin.

Joyful and intent, Laska started through the bog, which gave beneath her feet.

Running into the marsh, Laska at once detected all over the place, mingled with the familiar smells of roots, marsh grass, slime, and the extraneous odor of horse dung, the scent of birds—of that strong-smelling bird that always excited her more than any other. Here and there among the moss and swamp-sage this scent was very strong, but it was impossible to be sure in which direction it grew stronger or fainter. To find this out it was necessary to get farther to the lee of the wind. Scarcely aware of her legs under her, Laska bounded on with a stiff gallop, so that at each bound she could stop, going to the right, away from the morning breeze blowing from the east, and turned to face the wind. Sniffing in the air with dilated nostrils, she knew at once that not their scent only but they themselves were here before her, and not only one but a great many of them. Laska slackened her pace. They were here, but precisely where she could not yet decide. To find the exact spot, she began circling round, when suddenly her master's voice drew her off. "Laska! Here!" he called, pointing to the other side. She stood still, asking him if it would not be better to let her go on as she had begun. But he repeated his command in an angry voice, pointing to a tufty place under water, where there could not be anything. She obeyed, pretending to search, and to please him went over the whole place and then returned to the first spot, and was at once on the scent again. Now, when he was not hindering her, she knew what to do, and without looking where she was stepping, stumbling impatiently over hummocks and falling into water, but righting herself with her strong, supple legs, she began the circle that was to make everything clear. *Their* scent came to her more and more pungently, more and more distinctly, until all at once it became quite plain that one of them was here, on the other side of this tuft of reeds, five paces in front of her. She stopped and her whole body grew rigid. Her short legs prevented her from seeing ahead, but by the scent she was certain it was there, not five paces off. More and more conscious of its presence, she stood still, in the joy of anticipation. Her tail was stretched straight and tense, only the very tip twitching. Her mouth was slightly open, her ears pricked. One ear had got folded back when she was running. She breathed heavily but warily, and still more warily looked round, more with her eyes than her head, to her master. He was coming along, with his familiar face but ever terrible eyes, stumbling over the hummocks and taking to her an unusually long time. She thought he came slowly but in reality he was running.

From Laska's peculiar posture—her mouth half open and her body crouched down as if dragging her hind legs along the ground—Levin knew she was pointing at snipe, and with an inward prayer for success, especially with his first bird, he ran towards her. When he came up close to her and looked beyond, he saw from his height what she had perceived with her nose. In a little space between two hummocks he caught sight of a snipe. It had turned its head and was listening. Then lightly preening and folding its wings, it disappeared round a corner with an awkward jerk of its tail.

"Go, Laska, go!" shouted Levin, giving her a shove from behind.

"But I can't go," thought Laska. "Where am I to go? I can scent them from here, but if I move I shan't know where they are or what they are." But now he pushed her with his knee, and in an excited whisper said, "Go, Laska, good dog, go!"

"All right, if that's what he wants, but I can't answer for myself now," thought Laska, and rushed forward at full tilt between the hummocks. She was no longer on the scent, but only saw and heard, without understanding anything.

Ten paces from her former place a snipe rose with a guttural cry, its wings making the hollow sound peculiar to snipe. And immediately following the report it fell heavily on its white breast in the wet bog. Another rose behind Levin, without waiting to be put up by the dog. By the time Levin had turned towards it, it was already some way off. But his shot caught it. It flew on about twenty feet, rose sharply, and then, turning over and over like a ball, dropped heavily to the ground, on a dry spot.

"This looks like business!" thought Levin, stowing the warm fat snipe into his game-bag. "Eh, Laska, what do you think?"

When Levin had reloaded his gun and moved on, the sun, though still invisible behind the clouds, had already risen. The moon had lost all her splendor, and gleamed pale in the sky like a small cloud. There was no longer a single star to be seen. The sedge, silvery with dew before, now glistened like gold. The patches of rust were now amber. The bluish grass had turned a yellow-green. Marsh-birds bustled about in the bushes that sparkled with dew and cast long shadows beside the brook. A hawk woke up and settled on a haycock, turning its head from side to side and surveying the marsh with an air of discontent. Crows were flying about the field, and a barefooted boy was already driving the horses towards an old man, who had raised himself from under his coat and was scratching different parts of his body. The smoke from the gun stretched white as milk over the green grass.

One of the boys ran up to Levin.

"There were wild ducks here yesterday!" he shouted, following Levin at a distance.

And Levin knew a double pleasure in killing three more snipe, one after another, in sight of the boy, who expressed his approval.

# Bambi and Lassie

### Mary Clearman Blew

VERN WAS DEAD set on catching himself a pet fawn. All through the late winter at the supper table, under the bare electric light, tilting back in his chair with one boot heel cocked on a rung, grinning with the pleasure of talking in his monotonous cracked tenor, he rambled and repeated himself and always reverted back to the fawn. People he knew had raised several fawns, Vern said, and one of these days he was going to catch himself one.

"You leave them damn deer alone," my father said once, but Vern went on talking as if he hadn't heard him. I think, over the course of the year that he had worked for my father, that both of my parents had stopped listening to Vern. My mother would get up from the table and fill the dishpan and finally clear his plate and knife and fork from in front of him as though he wasn't there, but it never fazed him; he just kept talking as long as anybody else sat at the table.

Today I wonder, of all things, what Vern wanted with a pet fawn. He was nineteen, a grown man from my thirteen-year-old point of view, muscled under his dark blue pearl-snap shirt and his blue jeans, with a healthy head of dark hair and greenish, protuberant eyes over a long nose. He'd been raised deep in the foothills of the Snowy Mountains and hadn't been to school much, which was not that uncommon in remote Montana in the late nineteen fifties. Something about his family was unmentionable, although to this day I don't know what it was. But Vern was a good worker, dependable, with hardheaded ranch sense. He slept in an old Airstream trailer my father had set on blocks just outside the yard fence, and he ate his meals with us, and he gave his dirty clothes to my mother to wash in her old wringer washer, hang on the line to dry, sprinkle and iron, and give back to him. He helped in the dairy and with whatever ranch chores needed to be done, fencing, feeding sheep, tinkering to keep the truck and tractor running.

Because Vern was such a good worker, my father was able to load our whole family in the car after school was out in June and drive over to Washington State for the only vacation he and my mother ever took. When we came home, Vern had his fawn.

He'd found it, out there, somewhere, he said, waving a hand vaguely toward meadow, brush, and hillside cow pasture. It was a whitetail fawn, an orphan. The doe had gone off and left it. He was feeding it from one of the lamb's bottles. The fawn drank much like a lamb, butting and jerking its tail. My father just snorted and otherwise kept what he thought to himself, but my little sisters and I were enchanted. Deer, whitetail and mule deer, were almost as common as sheep in our foothills, but as peripheral pale dun shapes that drifted down into the hayfields at twilight, restless as ghosts and as easily startled back into the brush and timber. It was a novelty to stand near this fawn, close enough for once to count its spots and marvel at its tiny hooves and huge liquid eyes. It never stopped drinking milk from the bottle when we tried to pet it, but its flesh shrank away from our hands.

"What will we name it?" I asked. I had something romantic in mind, from my book reading.

"Oh, I thought I'd call him Bambi," said Vern, grinning as though he had just dreamed up the perfect name for a deer.

In ranch country there is always a right way to do things. To do otherwise is to be branded as an outsider, not very bright, and probably unreliable. To be an insider, of course, is to live within a lasso that tightens down through the community to the hard knot of a single family. In the Snowy Mountain foothills where I woke into the pains of adolescence, all buckskin horses were named Buck, all ring-necked shepherd dogs were Ring, and, unhappily, nearly everybody had a black cow or horse named Nig. Bambi was the right name to give to a fawn, just as Lassie was the right name to give to a collie dog. When I had pleaded with my father to give the dog a romantic name, or any name but Lassie, he had looked at me as though I had lost my mind.

"What else would you name a female collie dog?"

Deer hunting, of course, was a right thing to do. My father owned a 30.30 rifle, a .22, and a shotgun, the typical ranchman's arsenal in those days before black-powder pistols and single-shot rifles became fashionable. Like all ranch children, my sisters and I were taught to assume that every gun was loaded unless we personally had seen it unloaded, and we knew—knew automatically, knew religiously, like a kind of apostle's creed—never to point a gun at anything we didn't intend to shoot. We knew other right things, like never to shoot at anything we couldn't see clearly and never to shoot over a horizon. These right things to do were drilled so deeply into us that I cannot remember hearing them for the first time, and I always felt the kind of shock touched off by blasphemy to hear that somebody had done something stupid with a gun, inevitably *some damn guy from town.*

Still, the right thing to do in one ranch family may not be the right thing to do in another family. Where Vern was raised, shooting at the dog with the rifle when she didn't stop chasing the sheep when he called to her may have been the right thing to do, but it ruined the dog forever for work.

Lassie was a purebred collie that my father had purchased, actually paid money for, to replace our old stock dog. Collies, after all, were said to be the best dogs you could have for cattle and sheep. Lassie had a long gold and white coat that went ratty with spring mud and summer stickers, cockleburs and beggar's lice, and she had soulful dark eyes set deep in her narrow, overbred head. A cross word was enough to send her running to hide under the lilac bush back of the house.

I don't think I saw it. Months later, when my father fired Vern, I did hear my mother mutter under her breath that taking that shot at her was what ruined the dog, but I think I've imagined how Vern stormed, red-faced and righteous, into the built-on room we called the out-kitchen, grabbed the rifle from where it stood in the corner behind the wringer washer and the buckets of chicken feed and the winter coats hung on nails, threw a shell into it and stormed out again to take aim and fire over the dog's head into the side of the hill where, yapping mindlessly, she had chased the sheep up against the fence. I know I've imagined how the dirt exploded, the spray of shale almost simultaneous with the crack of the rifle, and how every muscle of Vern's body, long neck and sloping shoulders and prominent buttocks, vibrated with *the right thing to do.*

I had read *Bambi* by the time I was eight years old, the real novel by Felix Salten, not the later, sentimental version based on the Disney film, so I knew what the falling leaves said to each other, and how insects measured their tiny lifespans, and why a wounded fawn, nursed back to health by a human, lost his fear and consequently his life to the next hunter's bullet. This knowledge earned me a round of derisive familial laughter one frosty fall morning when I called after my father as he rode off with his rifle, "Remember! Just shoot the stags!"

*Stag*, of course, was the wrong word. The right word would have been *buck*.

Our Bambi might have grown up to be a buck if my father, growling to himself about the prospects of a full-grown buck deer with antlers living with us, hadn't snapped one of the rubber bands he used to castrate lambs on Bambi's testicles. So Bambi grew up a wether, not quite wild and not quiet tame. He watched our comings and goings with interest, and he would sail over the chicken-yard fence to eat the chickens' feed or slip into the barn to lip up the grain in the milk cows' mangers, but he dodged beyond our fingertips, his muscles writhing like snakes under his dun-colored pelt, shivering with revulsion if one of us did manage to touch him.

For all his life on the periphery, however, Bambi had a friend in Lassie, the collie.

I have never seen another interspecies attachment like theirs, although I have read about them, and a few years ago my sister had a gander, sole survivor of his flock after an attack by coyotes, who assuaged his need to be one of many by hanging out with the horses. It made a strange sight, ten or a dozen horses, grazing on the shale hillside in the shade of pines with the gander among them, nipping bunchgrass with his bill and serenely unconscious of any absurdity in the company he was keeping.

Attributing human feelings to animal behavior is risky, in part because any such attributions must be made in language. I don't suppose the gander thought of himself as part of a family whose other members were horses. And who can say what Bambi and Lassie thought, the fawn that had been stolen from his natural life and the dog whose inbreeding and ill treatment had deprived her of what natural wits she might have had, or whether the way they saw each other can be glossed by words like *thought* or *feelings*, let alone *friendship*. And yet how they seemed to enjoy each other's company as they played together in the graveled road between the house and the barn, Lassie panting and slavering and leaping, Bambi dancing on his hind legs as though *en pointe*, sparring with his forelegs, as they wove around the shed and the tractor and the root cellar in a patternless pattern.

And then—perhaps some sudden sound or movement, who knows—Bambi would be off, white tail like a flag, in a burst of bounding speed that left Lassie mid-dance, alone and bereft.

"She gets the funniest look when he does that," my father would say. "She must think he's a damned fast dog, and he probably thinks she's a damned slow deer."

Bambi belonged to us, almost as much as Lassie and the sheep and milk cows and horses belonged to us, and so did the nameless deer that slipped in and out of the timber at twilight to feed on the haystacks. True, any rancher who was caught shooting deer out of season by the game warden could expect a heavy fine or even a jail sentence, but the point was not to get caught. Long before I ever heard the libertarian argument for private ownership of wildlife, I understood the ranch creed. *The deer get fat on our alfalfa. In the winter they eat our hay. The way they multiply, hell, we're lousy with deer, especially them goddamn whitetail and the way they're crowding out the mule deer. There won't be a mulie left in this country in ten years. Only makes sense to thin out them whitetail.*

*After all, we eat all the venison we shoot.*

The main thing was not to talk about poaching, not to draw attention to ourselves. Deer hair on the tailgate of a neighbor's pickup, blood on somebody's clothes? Hell, they probably butchered a goat. Good eating, goat, especially when it's fat on alfalfa hay. And hard as times are, between the deer eating the hay and the price they're paying for butterfat, a man can't hardly make a living on a dairy. He's got a right to eat, don't he? And feed his kids? Hell, even the game warden won't go out of his way to catch a rancher poaching, not unless he's some educated fool they brought in from Fish and Game, *from outside*. Remember the story Brownie told, Brownie that used to live on that place below the butte? He'd shot his deer and was dressing it out when he heard somebody whistling and calling his dog on the other side of the hill, "Here Spot, here Spot." Brownie just gets his deer good and hid when over the hill comes the game warden, and hell, he doesn't have no dog with him. He was just giving Brownie plenty of time to hide the evidence.

We ate venison all year around, varied only by fried chicken from my mother's flock. Venison steaks, roasts, and round meat patties broiled the way my father liked them, rosy rare. There was no doubt in our minds that it was the right thing to do.

And so hunting in the foothills was never for sport. Nobody, after all, had time for mere fun. Hunting was for meat. If it was for more than meat, it was for closing the circle around us, like a good fence.

Fun was something that children were expected to grow out of, but the summer I was thirteen I began to desire more from life than

I was getting. It wasn't so much movies and allowances and clothes like the town girls wore that I was longing for, although of course I longed for these things, too, but rather a sense that I was ready for something that wasn't happening and that was far likelier to be happening in the great outside world than within the hard knot of family. My longing was what led to my driving lessons from Vern in my father's jeep, up and down the mountain dirt roads with one of my little sisters crammed beside us in the front seat and watching me sideways when Vern's hand came to be clamped between my legs to feel me through my blue jeans. It was my first experience of anything of the kind, and my skin crawled with revulsion, but I didn't know what to do except suddenly to steer the jeep straight for a cut-bank so he'd have to take his hand away to steer back in the road. But his hand always came back, clamped even more firmly in place.

The blow-up came that summer when some of the lambs got into the Airstream where Vern slept, and he blamed me for—what—leaving the door open, maybe, or going in the Airstream and messing with his stuff—and he yelled at me, and my mother heard him, and that and my little sister's sardonic eyes led to my tearful confession, in the kitchen, that Vern had been putting his hand between my legs and I didn't like it.

After the enormous silence my mother said only, "I'll take care of it, and your dad don't have to know all of it."

Vern cried when my father fired him. ("Won't have you yelling at my kids," was how my mother reported my father's exact words.)

And, "You've been better to me than my own father," my mother reported Vern saying, before he packed his stuff in his red pickup and drove off. The dairy wasn't doing well enough, anyway, for my father to afford to pay a hired man, and Vern's work would fall on my mother's shoulders and mine.

Bambi lived with us, or near us, for several years, playing with Lassie until she got too decrepit, wandering farther and showing up less frequently to eat the chickens' feed. Then one summer a kid my father had hired to stack bales borrowed his rifle one twilight and went out to shoot some fresh meat. He came back with his deer and a funny look on his face. "Thought I was killing a doe," he said, "but when I went to dress it out, it wasn't."

Now when I remember Vern, and the stolen fawn and the abused dog and the molested child, I wonder what he was hunting for, and I speculate that it was for his place in the world, however small, where he could claim sovereignty. One of too many children growing up on a scrap of a ranch embedded deep in poor mountain soil, with no chance for land of his own, knowing nothing but ranch work, he had moved in with us and brought his expectations along with his pickup truck and his few changes of clothes. He may have thought my adolescent behavior was an invitation, or at least an opportunity. He probably didn't think that a thirteen-year-old was still a child, but he didn't know that I was already old enough to look down on his table manners and the way he hunted for his fork when I set the supper table the way it was set in town, with the fork on the left-hand side of the plate instead of being lined up the ranch way with the knife and spoon on the right.

At thirteen I was already dreaming my escape from the ranch. Where, I didn't know, the movies, maybe. Today I realize that certain articles of the old creed have been drilled into me for life; an unwilled contempt for sentimentality (oh yes, we butchered Bambi and cooked and ate him, without a qualm); secret embarrassment for those who act out ancient hunting rituals with blood smeared on their cheeks; sudden rage when I read in the Spokane newspaper about the hunter who, thinking he heard a bear, fired into the bushes and badly wounded his neighbor, who had been taking a Sunday afternoon walk with his wife. The old voices turn up their volume: *Some damn guy from town. The son of a bitch, shooting where he can't see. Somebody ought to take him out and shoot him. It's bastards like him that give them goddamn legislators an excuse to take our guns away from us . . .*

At thirteen I was as unaware as Vern that, in future years, *the right thing to do* would take on so many permutations, until all I can be sure of is the beauty of the patternless pattern that Bambi wove when he danced with Lassie, *en pointe* on his hind legs, flashing his forelegs at her as she leaped and slavered, through the wild hawthorns in white wet spring bloom, her coat drenched, shedding raindrops, dragging pine needles, their noses touching at the strange edges of their transparent boundaries, their legs inter-twined in what to any human observer looked like love, until, his eyes liquid and fathomless, her eyes perplexed and bewildered, the unheard sound, the unseen motion, sent him bounding, his tail a white flag, into the shadows of all that has passed, the shelter of the pines.

# Part Five

*It is painful to witness the death of the smallest of God's created beings, much more, one in which life is so vigorously maintained as the Whale! And when I saw this, the largest and most terrible of all created animals bleeding, quivering, dying a victim to the cunning of man, my feelings were indeed peculiar!*

—Enoch Cloud
LIFE ON A WHALESHIP, 1851–1854

# PUTTING FISH BACK

## Roderick Haig-Brown

I DECIDED TO wonder the other day just how many fish a year I kill to make my sport. So I looked back over the records, missing out most of the war years and stopping short of those years when I was working hard to try and learn about fish—how they grow, when they spawn, what they feed on, why they are fat or lean or dark or light. The answer seems to be, from ten to twenty steelheads, summer and winter; about a dozen salmon, a little less than fifty cutthroat and rainbow trout.

These are not big figures. I knew a man who used to kill every year over a thousand trout in two months' fishing on a big lake; later in the year he used to kill around three hundred salmon, sometimes in catches of thirty or forty in a single day. He always fished from a boat, always with a fly, usually with two rods. And he liked to kill fish. I think he was nuts; he thought I was nuts. If the point of going fishing is to catch and kill fish, undoubtedly he was right. If the point of going fishing is to have a good time with a minimum of destruction, maybe I have a point.

Even so, my figures are probably larger than they need be. Having a wife and four children who like to eat fish, I undoubtedly kill a few each year that might otherwise have been turned back. And I still occasionally kill a fish because I want to learn something about him that I do not think I can learn in any other way.

It is reasonable to ask at this point: why such reluctance in a professed fisherman to kill fish? The main reason, I suppose, is that I don't enjoy killing anything, so I cannot see that doing so adds to the sport of going fishing. But I also have the feeling that there are not and cannot be enough fish of the kinds I am mainly interested in to go around the steadily increasing numbers of anglers. I know there are places where trout are so numerous that a heavy intensity of fishing is needed to keep them at a worthwhile size and prevent deterioration of their food resources; but I do not often fish such places, and if I did so I should feel reasonably certain that there would be plenty of other fishermen all too willing to apply the necessary pressure.

Really worthwhile fish, like migratory cutthroats and rainbows, Atlantic salmon, Pacific salmon and non-migratory trout of good size, are nowhere so numerous that they threaten their own future. They are nowhere sufficiently numerous to withstand unlimited fishing. And only rarely—never in waters easily accessible by road—are they able to hold their own against the determination of anglers to kill them, and of industry to poison them or bar them out or dry up their water supply. If one is convinced of this, as I am, some thought of limiting one's own killing is inevitable.

The first and most obvious limitation is by method—limiting oneself to artificial lures only or to fly only or to particularly fine tackle—and from this there is an immediate gain in improved sport. But it does not go far enough; fly only, even dry fly only, in the right hands and under the right conditions can kill a lot of fish as my fly-fishing friend showed when he counted his trout by thou sands and his salmon by hundreds. Nor are the legal limits set on anglers by states and provinces even nearly good enough, as is clearly shown by their periodic downward revision as fishing intensity increases and the yields of sport grow slim. I have seen the British Columbia bag limit of trout reduced from twenty-four to fifteen to twelve within the space of twenty years, and I shall undoubtedly see it reduced still further. And almost as surely, good fishing within the reduced limits will become harder and harder to find.

I think the wise fisherman, who knows what is good for the present and future of his sport, usually pays little attention to the size limits or the bag limits allowed by most game commissions. Six, or at least eight inches, is the usual minimum size limit for trout. But I have yet to see a six- or eight-inch trout that was worth a sportsman's while, except to fill an immediate, frying-pan need; even nine- and ten-inch trout are pathetically small fish and I'm inclined to think that from a fisherman's point of view a trout hardly becomes a trout until it is at least ten inches long; below that size it is a creature of promise, not fulfillment.

I find I develop rather quickly a clear idea of what kind of trout I want from almost any water. Usually I can say I don't want anything smaller than twelve inches, and stay faithfully enough to that. Occasionally I settle for ten; more often fourteen seems about right. There is a sort of relationship here between size and numbers; roughly, I should say, twelve ten-inch trout make a good bag, or eight twelve-inchers, or six fourteen-inch fish. Which doesn't mean one has to go all out to kill such limits or must necessarily stop at them if they are below legal limits; simply that they are good controls to keep in mind. As often as not a brace of fourteen- or sixteen-inch fish are plenty to bring home; occasionally, for some special purpose, one may need a few more. But to kill a legal limit of fish every time it is possible to do so seems to me the height of folly and waste.

There are other ways of setting one's own limits. I shall never again kill three winter steelhead in one day, for instance, because I think that is too many, even though the law allows it. Two is a better limit and one is all I usually bring home. One Coho salmon is all I ever want from a stream in a day's fishing—if the fish happen to be taking well it is quite easy to turn them loose. Half a dozen sea-run cutthroats are enough for me or any other man in one day; estuary fish are too accessible for common sense to permit more killing than that.

I fish a good deal in one big lake that has seven tributary streams, all of which are good. Most of the streams are widely separated, and by rowboat it is a minor feat to fish more than two or three of them in a single day. With an outboard one can reach them all and fish them all within twelve or fourteen hours, and occasionally it is pleasant to do so. But there is an obvious obligation to recognize the improved transportation by some sort of limit. The one I have found most interesting is a limit of not more than one fish from each creek, the fish to be not less than fourteen inches and taken on a floating fly. It is not an easy limit to achieve, because one is almost certain to find at least one creek where the fish are determinedly off their feeding. And it is a limit that is certainly not going to harm anything if it is achieved.

But all bag limits are evil if they are regarded as a mark to fish for or shoot at, and this is almost invariably what happens to them. They are set as control, as a maximum not to be exceeded. Instead of using them in this way the hunter or fisherman tends to use them as a minimum measure of his sport; "I got my limit in a couple of hours," he will say. Or, if things didn't work out that well he will come home almost ashamed to admit that his skill has not yielded him every last measure of death the law allows, regardless of whether his day has been a good one. I have two hopes for the future. The first and lesser one is that game commissions will one day have sense enough to set limits that measurably reflect the sport safety available. The second and deeply urgent one is that we shall grow a race of sportsmen no one of whom will ever consider it a matter for pride to have killed a limit.

The fisherman's enormous advantage in the matter of bag limits is that he can limit his killing without appreciably limiting his sport, and he can also select what he does kill in a way that is seldom possible in other sports. True, the big game hunter can select for head or size with care; the duck hunter can wait for certain species and limit himself to drakes only. But once the shot is fired the choice is made and there is no release from it for hunter or hunted. The fisherman can throw his fly, rise and hook and play his fish, even net him or beach him or hold him in his hands—and still return him unharmed to life.

It is often claimed that it is difficult to return a fish safely to the water. I am satisfied that it is not. A little knowledge is necessary, a little understanding of how a fish works, and a few reasonably precise and confident hand movements. Fish that have been netted will not die, as some people believe, "because the mesh has cut the slime and exposed the fish to disease." Fish handled with dry hands will not die from this alone. Fish dropped back into the water from a reasonable height will not die. These are tales spread by men who want an excuse for killing all the fish they catch, and experience simply does not bear them out.

As a generalization, it is safe to say that the smaller a fish is, the easier it is to give him his freedom. He will not exhaust himself so much as a larger fish, the hook frees more readily from his softer mouth, and his smaller body seems to react more promptly to renewed flow of water through his gills. It is also true that while a fly-fisherman should be able to release safely very nearly a hundred per cent of the fish he hooks, a bait fisherman cannot hope to do nearly so well because of the tendency of the fish to take the bait farther down into their throats.

One of the most important rules in releasing fish is to do so with a minimum of handling. I have released hundreds of fish, including salmon and steelhead, without ever taking them out of the water—simply by reaching down, gripping the shank of the hook and twisting it out. This is hard on the fly, but never on the fish. When a fish must be handled, it is best to hold him by the tail or lower jaw if possible, and still without taking him out of the water. But I have freed many good-sized trout by netting them, lifting them out of the net by the lower jaw, freeing the hook with my other hand, then putting them gently back in the water, using an easy hold on tail or body with the second hand only after they are in the water.

The danger in handling fish is not, it seems, in the warmth or dryness of the hand, but in exerting pressure that damages vital organs. Some years ago I read of an experiment that tested the relative safety of handling fish with wet or dry hands. Of large numbers of fish handled in both ways, the percentage survival of those handled with dry hands was considerably greater, and the conclusion was that the greater pressure necessary to hold fish in wet hands had damaged vital organs and so caused the higher mortality. That is why I feel sure a minimum of handling is desirable and why I believe that pressure, when necessary, is best applied at the wrist of the tail, on the back or on the lower jaw.

A fish that has lost a considerable amount of blood probably will not survive; fish have small hearts and the blood circulates slowly and at low pressure, so there is not much blood to be lost. A fish that cannot hold itself upright and swim away probably will not survive, especially if it is a large fish. Large fish like steelheads and salmon must often be completely exhausted before they can be beached and freed from the hook. To give them a chance it is essential to hold them upright in the stream while they gulp some water through their gills and regain enough oxygen to strengthen themselves. If they are slow to do this, it pays to draw them gently back and forth through the water to start the gills moving. Usually they will swim away after less than a minute of this treatment, but I have released them and grabbed them again to continue the treatment when they seemed unable to hold an even keel. I have never found again a fish that swam strongly away from me; I don't think I have ever failed to find again one that could not regain enough strength to hold itself upright, though I have sometimes left them in sheltered water in the hope they would recover.

The test of the survival of fish that have been handled is in the return of the thousands upon thousands of fish that have been marked or tagged. And any fisherman who wants to convince himself of the recuperative powers of fish has only to remember those he has caught with the healed scars of formidable wounds. I have caught healed and healthy fish whose eyes or jaws or both had been torn away by hooks, fish whose whole bodies were deeply net-scarred, fish so deeply bitten by seals and other predators that they seemed deformed. The prick of a hook, a few minutes of dancing on the end of a line, the gentle handling of skillful release, will not kill creatures designed to survive the batterings of a dangerous lifetime.

# DEATH ON THE MUSSELSHELL
## John Holt

IT WASN'T PARTICULARLY large as brown trout go in this central Montana river. Perhaps fourteen inches and plump. A perfect fit for the cast iron skillet back at camp. So I grasped the fish around its belly and whacked its head on a streamside rock, the sound of the killing blow sounding like the muted *thwack* of a baseball bat making solid contact with a fastball grooved right down the pipe. The brown quivered in my hand for a few seconds, then stilled, the body lifeless, bright yellow and walnut hues already starting to fade, eye glazed in death.

My friend watched the scene from the bank and asked, "Why'd you kill it instead of releasing it, or anyway putting it in the creel?"

"Death is death. He was played out and chances are he would have gone belly up even if I put him back in the river. This ends the suffering fast and killing them this way preserves the flavor. We have to eat, too." I placed the dead brown in my old wicker creel. "When they flop around in there and die slowly, lactic acid builds in the muscle tissues and sours the flesh. Sour trout isn't to my liking."

John Glisch and I had broken into the newspaper game together many long years ago and during his stretch as one of this country's last real newsmen he'd covered the cops for a paper in Las Vegas, so he'd pretty much seen it all when it came to death and suffering. Still, when I glanced up at him I noticed a look of something approaching pained perplexity.

"What gives, man?" I asked.

"Hell Holt, I like my trout sweet too," and he laughed. "But it was almost like you enjoyed killing that brown . . . in a twisted way."

I had to think on that one for a bit. When catch-and-release fishing—the sometimes artful fooling of a fish with a fly and a skillful presentation, the playing of that fish and then its careful release back into its watery environment—first came into vogue over twenty years ago I was all for it. I was in favor of anything that preserved and even enhanced any fishery. I went for almost five years without killing anything. Trout, bass, northern pike, even carp, escaped my frying pan. What's more, I stopped hunting sharptailed grouse in the coulee-and-bluff country of southeastern Montana, land that I care for more than myself. And I preached the gospel according to Barbless Hook at anyone within earshot.

Catch-and-release was the only way. Anyone killing fish for the pan or a trophy was a barbarian in my narrow-focused eyes.

Time passed and I religiously turned free thousands of fish that I briefly captured from the many glorious rivers in Montana and Alberta and from the lakes of interior Iceland and the Muskie waters of Wisconsin. I'd become a zealot. When the fight with a truly large sporting fish lasted ten minutes or more I would carefully unhook the fish and then very slowly move it back and forth in calm water, hoping to infuse oxygen into its gills and thus into its bloodstream

When a given fish finally quivered back to some semblance of life and would then swim slowly away, sinking into the dark depths of a river or lake to sulk, a feeling passed through me of having done the right thing. I felt like a fine and goodhearted man.

As the pursuit of fish with a fly passed from being something looked upon by other anglers (bait, spin and what-not) as a harmless and often futile eccentricity, and fly-fishing moved on—thanks largely to the impetus of *A River Runs Through It,* especially the movie version—into the realm of full-tilt marketeering that it is today, one of the big attractions for the recently-monied, youthful arbitrageurs was that they could catch their fish and release them alive, too. That glorious 22-inch rainbow that leaped and crashed its way down the Beaverhead on a blustery October afternoon would live to fight again. And the catcher of that fish could go for years claiming that not only was he a skilled angler, but he was also a true sportsman. He released his fish. Killing wasn't his style. He wasn't a slob spinfisher who caught a mess of bluegills for the family dinner. Or way down the angling chain, a lowly, boorish baitfisher who resorted to loathsome worms or half-dead minnows impaled on a hook.

Well, bullshit. I've come to realize that all fishing is baitfishing. What do we think a trout takes a #22 Blue Wing Olive for? Does a five-pound brown really think that my tiny mélange of dubbing, hackle and thread is a work of art deserving detailed examination? No. That fish is after food. Nothing more. Nothing less. I've never really understood why such large fish make fools of themselves, delicately sipping a bug that may provide all of one calorie of food value. But clearly they're hungry.

Bait is bait whether it is feather and yarn, earthworm, or dough-ball. Fish aren't in any of this for sport. Neither are most of the river guides anymore.

Used to be they were largely a tough, no-nonsense lot, cantankerous to a fare-thee-well, who loved to fish almost as much as they loved to slug cheap bourbon. The new millennium version of a river guide claims to be a skilled fisheries biologist, entomologist, consummate outdoorsman, and God's gift to flyfishing. Many of them truly believe deep down in their hearts that old-time anglers like Lee Wulff and A. J. McClane were rank amateurs. True, many of them do indeed know it all, and can cast like Renoir painted. And they're dressed to prove it, in gaudy electric blues, reds, and greens, or pastel shades with names I can't even pronounce. Often, just to show that they're regular guys (or gals) they wear old, baggy, patched waders. Though they're sanctimonious about catch-and-release, they think nothing of floating over the same stretch of holding water a hundred times a year and nailing the same beleaguered fish as many times, leaving the hapless creature hook-scarred, underfed, and thus emaciated come autumn—unable to survive the hard winter ahead.

How does this connect with killing versus catch-and-release? Simple. The concept of releasing a fish after it was fooled, played, and then played out was and still is to some extent a good one. After all, killing 20, 30, or 100 fish a day will destroy even the best fishery in no time. But guides are now in the numbers game. They make their money and tips on their reputations for putting "clients" onto large numbers of large fish, and send them away and boasting that they returned alive everything they caught.

I live near the Yellowstone River. I watch as the Avon armada of skilled and unskilled guides drift their "sports" downstream day after day in season. When I walk the banks of the river near evening after this onslaught I notice dead or dying trout floating belly up in slow-circling eddies and calm places near shore. Ten inch rainbows. Fifteen inch cutthroats. Twenty inch browns.

Yes, some of the released fish live to fight another day, but not the 90 percent claimed by most guides, industry shills and even many biologists. Try 50 percent, or a more realistic 30.

I've watched baitfishers over the years and most of them kill only enough fish for a good dinner, maybe six or eight. True, some slaughter dozens, but they're in a minority. Let's say one of the artful anglers and his more artful guide float a Montana river and take 50 trout—browns, rainbows, brooks, whatever—and release all of them. They will go home thinking that 90% percent of those fish lived. Well, even if true, that means five fish died. That's an optimistic scenario. More than likely half of those trout—25 of them—went belly up before sundown, and perhaps as many as 35. Pretty simple math here.

But that doesn't get to the soul of the matter. The attraction of fishing is visceral and primal, genetically programmed into us from way back in our hunter/gatherer beginnings when meat brought home to the cave or wickiup meant living to hunt, fish, make love, or fight another day. Forget all this high-flown nonsense that says, "I fish to experience the land and all its wonders. I love to fully experience the riparian corridor." I feel the same way about good country, but when I cast a Joe's Hopper tight to the bank above a feeding brown I want to connect with that wild fish, feel the rush that comes from its all-out fight for survival. I'm a predator and a meat eater, and I've still got the teeth to prove it.

I'm with the Inuit and the Dene of the Yukon and Northwest Territories on how they feel about this issue. To catch fish and not kill and eat any of them is both disrespectful to the fish and a betrayal of the angler's heart. Don't get me wrong, though. Catch-and-release *does* help maintain a fishery in some overworked waters, and in these situations it has its place. But you won't find me on those waters anymore. To go through an entire angling life without consciously killing a single fish, without taking full responsibility for that life and death, and without eating that fish, is a tame, unconscious, disconnected approach to flyfishing—a juiceless, frightened, and sometimes arrogant way to go about connecting with nature.

So several years ago I finally realized that I was fishing more and enjoying it less. I decided to keep a few fish to eat each season. In part because they're good to eat and also to get back in touch with the life-and-death aspects of the sport. I now fish less than I used to but have regained the enjoyment I'd lost in my self-righteous days. And every time I kill a fish I experience a sense of awe bordering on downright fear about how serious even the "fun" aspects really are. The best of life puts me in touch with how transitory and insignificant all of what I do is. Killing a brown trout on the Musselshell River, as the ageless Crazy Mountains stare down at me with utter indifference, is a humbling, valuable experience.

When I looked up from creeling the fish I'd just killed, my friend Glisch was bringing a decent brown to shore. Sixteen inches, I guessed. He dropped to his knees in the water, flailed around trying to grab the thrashing trout, and struggled to twist the hook from its jaw. Then, holding this brown, he paused for a moment before turning to a slab of rock next to him. He raised the brown to shoulder height, like some kind of offering to the sky gods, and I watched the sunlight sparkle on the trout's radiant flanks. Then, with both hands, he brought its head down hard on the stone.

*Thwack.*

I saw it shiver and die.

He turned to me and his eyes were alive with both sadness and insight, the awe that comes from killing, and the beginning of a new awareness about what fishing can really be. Life and death on the river mirrors the dance we stagger through everywhere else. Ending the life of that one brown trout changed things for my friend.

"Killing them rather than putting them back," he said, "—it isn't the same thing, is it?"

"No, it isn't."

# Part Six

*To exterminate or destroy animals by an invincible and automatic procedure is not hunting. Let me be absolutely clear: I do not mean that this would not be hunting for sport. No, no; the fact is that it would not be hunting at all. Hunting is something else, something more delicate.*

—José Ortega y Gassett
MEDITATIONS ON HUNTING (1942)

From

# OUT OF AFRICA

## Isak Dinesen

ON A NEW YEAR'S morning, before sunrise, Denys and I found ourselves on the new Narok Road, driving along as fast as we could go on a rough road.

Denys, the day before, had lent a heavy rifle to a friend of his who was going South with a shooting party, and late in the night he remembered that he had neglected to explain to him a certain trick in the rifle, by which the hair-trigger might be put out of action. He was worried about it and afraid that the hunter would come to some sort of harm by his ignorance. We could then think of no better remedy than that we should start as early as possible, take the new road and try to overtake the shooting party at Narok. It was sixty miles, through some rough country; the Safari was traveling by the old road and would be going slowly as it had heavy loaded lorries with it. Our only trouble was that we did not know if the new road would have been brought through all the way to Narok.

The early morning air of the African highlands is of such a tangible coldness and freshness that time after time the same fancy there comes back to you: you are not on earth but in dark deep waters, going ahead along the bottom of the sea. It is not even certain that you are moving at all, the flows of chilliness against your face may be the deep-sea currents, and your car, like some sluggish electric fish, may be sitting steadily upon the bottom of the Sea, staring in front of her with the glaring eyes of her lamps, and letting the submarine life pass by her. The stars are so large because they are no real stars but reflections, shimmering upon the surface of the water. Alongside your path on the sea-bottom, live things, darker than their surroundings, keep on appearing, jumping up and sweeping into the long grass, as crabs and beach-fleas will make their way into the sand. The light gets clearer, and, about sunrise, the sea-bottom lifts itself towards the surface, a new created island. Whirls of smells drift quickly past you, fresh rank smells of the olive-bushes, the brine scent of burnt grass, a sudden quelling smell of decay.

Kanuthia, Denys's boy, who sat in the back of the box-body car, gently touched my shoulder and pointed to the right. To the side of the road, twelve or fifteen yards away from it, was a dark bulk, a Manatee taking a rest on the sands, and on the top of it something was stirring in the dark water. It was, I saw later, a big dead Giraffe bull, that had been shot two or three days before. You are not allowed to shoot the Giraffe, and Denys and I later had to defend ourselves against the charge of having killed this one, but we could prove that it had been dead some time when we came upon it, though it was never found by whom or why it had been killed. Upon the huge carcass of the Giraffe, a lioness had been feeding, and now raised her head and shoulder above it to watch the passing car.

Denys stopped the car, and Kanuthia lifted the rifle, that he carried, off his shoulder. Denys asked me in a low voice, "Shall I shoot her?"—For he very courteously looked on the Ngong Hill as my private hunting-ground.—We were going across the land of the same Masai who had been to my house to bewail the loss of their cattle; if this was the animal which had killed one after the other of their cows and calves, the time had come to put an end to her. I nodded.

He jumped from the car and slid back a few steps, at the same moment the lioness dived down behind the body of the Giraffe, he ran round the Giraffe to get within shot of her, and fired. I did not see her fall; when I got out and up to her she was lying dead in a big black pool.

There was no time to skin her, we must drive on if we were to cut off the Safari at Narok. We gazed round and took note of the place, the smell of the dead Giraffe was so strong that we could not very well pass it unknowingly.

But when we had driven a further two miles there was no more road. The tools of the road-laborers lay here; on the other side of them was the wide stony land, just gray in the dawn, all unbroken by any touch of man. We looked at the tools and at the country, we would have to leave Denys's friend to take his chance with the rifle. Afterwards, when he came back, he told us that he had never had an opportunity to use it. So we turned back, and as we turned we got our faces to the Eastern sky, reddening over the plains and the hills. We drove towards it and talked all the time of the lioness.

The Giraffe came within view, and by this time we could see him clearly and distinguish,—where the light fell on to his side,—the darker square spots on his skin. And as we came near to him we saw that there was a lion standing on him. In approaching we were a little lower than the carcass; the lion stood straight up over it, dark, and behind him the sky was now all aflame. *Lion Passant Or.* A bit of his mane was lifted by the wind. I rose up in the car, so strong was the impression that he made, and Denys at that said: "You shoot this time." I was never keen to shoot with his rifle, which was too long and heavy for me, and gave me a bad shock; still here the shot was a declaration of love, should the rifle not then be of the biggest caliber? As I shot it seemed to me that the lion jumped straight up in the air, and came down with his legs gathered under him. I stood, panting, in the grass, aglow with the plenipotence that a shot gives you, because you take effect at a distance. I walked round the carcass of the Giraffe. There it was,—the fifth act of a classic tragedy. They were all dead now. The Giraffe was looking terribly big, austere, with his four stiff legs and long stiff neck, his belly torn open by the lions. The lioness, lying on her back, had a great haughty snarl on her face, she was the *femme fatale* of the tragedy. The lion was lying not far from her, and how was it that he had learned nothing by her fate? His head was laid on his two front paws, his mighty mane covered him as a royal mantle, he too was resting in a big pool, and by now the morning air was so light that it showed scarlet.

Denys and Kanuthia pulled up their sleeves and while the sun rose they skinned the lions. When they took a rest we had a bottle of claret, and raisins and almonds, from the car; I had brought them with us to eat on the road, because it was New Year's Day. We sat on the short grass and ate and drank. The dead lions, close by, looked magnificent in their nakedness, there was not a particle of superfluous fat on them, each muscle was a bold controlled curve, they needed no cloak, they were, all through, what they ought to be.

As we sat there, a shadow hastened over the grass and over my feet, and looking up I could distinguish, high in the light-blue sky, the circling of the vultures. My heart was as light as if I had been flying it, up there, on a string, as you fly a kite. I made a poem:

The eagle's shadow runs across the plain,
Towards the distant, nameless, air-blue mountains.
But the shadows of the round young Zebra
Sit close between their delicate hoofs all day,
    where they stand immovable,
And wait for the evening, wait to stretch out, blue,
Upon a plain, painted brick-red by the sunset,
And to wander to the water-hole.


Denys and I had another dramatic adventure with lions. It happened, in reality, before the other, in the early days of our friendship.

One morning, during the spring-rains, Mr. Nichols, a South African, who was then my Manager, came to my house all aflame, to tell me, that in the night two lions had been to the farm and had killed two of our oxen. They had broken through the fence of the oxen's fold, and they had dragged the dead oxen into the coffee plantation; one of them they had eaten up there, but the other was lying amongst the coffee-trees. Would I now write him a letter to go and get strychnine in Nairobi? He would have it laid out in the carcass at once, for he thought that the lions would be sure to come back in the night.

I thought it over; it went against me to lay out strychnine for lions, and I told him that I could not see my way to do it. At that his excitement changed over into exasperation. The lions, he said, if they were left in peace over this crime, would come back another time. The bullocks they had killed were our best working bullocks, and we could not afford to lose any more. The stable of my ponies, he reminded me, was not far from the oxen's enclosure, had I thought of that? I explained that I did not mean to keep the lions on the farm, only I thought that they should be shot and not poisoned.

"And who is going to shoot them?" asked Nichols, "I am no coward, but I am a married man and I have no wish to risk my life unnecessarily." It was true that he was no coward, he was a plucky little man. "There would be no sense in it," he said. No, I said, I did not mean to make him shoot the lions. But Mr. Finch-Hatton had arrived the night before and was in the house, he and I would go. "Oh, that is O.K." said Nichols.

I then went in to find Denys. "Come now," I said to him, "and let us go and risk our lives unnecessarily. For if they have got any value at all it is this that they have got none. *Frei lebt wer sterben kann.*"

We went down and found the dead bullock in the coffee plantation, as Nichols had told me; it had hardly been touched by the lions. Their spoor was deep and clear in the soft ground, two big lions had been here in the night. It was easy to follow through the plantation and up to the wood round Belknap's house, but by the time that we came there it had rained so heavily that it was difficult to see anything, and in the grass and the bush at the edge of the wood we lost the track.

"What do you think, Denys," I asked him, "will they come back tonight?"

Denys had great experience with lions. He said that they would come back early in the night to finish the meat, and that we ought to give them time to settle down on it, and go down to the field ourselves at nine o'clock. We would have to use an electric torch from his Safari outfit, to shoot by, and he gave me the choice of the rôles, but I would rather let him shoot and myself hold the torch for him.

In order that we might find our way up to the dead ox in the dark, we cut up strips of paper and fastened them on the rows of coffee-trees between which we meant to walk, marking our way in the manner of Hanzl and Gretl with their little white stones. It would take us straight to the kill, and at the end of it, twenty yards from the carcass, we tied a larger piece of paper to the tree, for here we would stop, sweep the light on and shoot. Late in the afternoon, when we took out the torch to try it, we found that the batteries of it had been running down and that the light it gave was only faint. There was no time to go in to Nairobi with it now, so that we should have to make the best of it as it was.

It was the day before Denys's birthday, and while we dined, he was in a melancholic mood, reflecting that he had not had enough out of life till now. But something, I consoled him, might still happen to him before his birthday morning. I told Juma to get out a bottle of wine to be ready for us when we should come back. I kept on thinking of the lions, where would they be now, at this moment? Were they crossing the river, slowly, silently, the one in front of the other, the gentle cold flow of the river turning round their chests and flanks?

At nine o'clock we went out.

It rained a little, but there was a moon; from time to time she put out her dim white face high up in the sky, behind layers and layers of thin clouds, and was then dimly mirrored in the white-flowering coffee-field. We passed the school at a distance; it was all lighted up.

At this sight a great wave of triumph and of pride in my people swept through me. I thought of King Solomon, who says: "The slothful man saith, There is a lion in the way; a lion is in the streets." Here were two lions just outside their door, but my school-children were not slothful and had not let the lions keep them from school.

We found our marked two rows of coffee-trees, paused a moment, and proceeded up between them, one in front of the other. We had moccasins on, and walked silently. I began to shake and tremble with excitement, I dared not come too near to Denys for fear that he might feel it and send me back, but I dared not keep too far away from him either, for he might need my torchlight any moment.

The lions, we found afterwards, had been on the kill. When they heard us, or smelt us, they had walked off it a little way into the coffee-field to let us pass. Probably because they thought that we were passing too slowly, the one of them gave a very low hoarse growl, in front and to the right of us. It was so low that we were not even sure that we had heard it, Denys stopped a second; without turning he asked me: "Did you hear?" "Yes," I said.

We walked a little again and the deep growling was repeated, this time straight to the right. "Put on the light," Denys said. It was not altogether an easy job, for he was much taller than I, and I had to get the light over his shoulder on to his rifle and further on. As I lighted the torch the whole world changed into a brilliantly lighted stage, the wet leaves of the coffee-trees shone, the clods of the ground showed up quite clearly.

First the circle of light struck a little wide-eyed jackal, like a small fox; I moved it on, and there was the lion. He stood facing us straight, and he looked very light, with all the black African night behind him. When the shot fell, close to me, I was unprepared for it, even without comprehension of what it meant, as if it had been thunder, as if I had been myself shifted into the place of the lion. He went down like a stone. "Move on, move on," Denys cried to me. I turned the torch further on, but my hand shook so badly that the circle of light, which held all the world, and which I commanded, danced a dance. I heard Denys laugh beside me in the dark.—"The torch-work on the second lion," he said to me later, "was a little shaky."—But in the center of the dance was the second lion, going away from us and half hidden by a coffee-tree. As the light reached him he turned his head and Denys shot. He fell out of the circle, but got up and into it again, he swung round towards us, and just as the second shot fell, he gave one long irascible groan.

Africa, in a second, grew endlessly big, and Denys and I, standing upon it, infinitely small. Outside our torchlight there was nothing but darkness, in the darkness in two directions there were lions, and from the sky rain. But when the deep roar died out, there was no movement anywhere, and the lion lay still, his head turned away on to his side, as in a gesture of disgust. There were two big dead animals in the coffee-field, and the silence of night all around.

We walked up to the lions and paced out the distance. From where we had stood the first lion was thirty yards away and the other twenty-five. They were both full-grown, young, strong, fat lions. The two close friends, out in the hills or on the plains, yesterday had taken the same great adventure into their heads, and in it they had died together.

By now all the school children were coming out of the school, pouring down the road to stop in sight of us and there to cry out in a low soft voice: "Msabu. Are you there? Are you there? Msabu, Msabu."

I sat on a lion and cried back to them: "Yes I am."

Then they went on, louder and more boldly: "Has Bedâr shot the lions? Both two?" When they found that it was so, they were at once all over the place, like a swarm of small spring-hares of the night, jumping up and down. They, then and there, made a song upon the event; it ran as follows: "Three shots. Two lions. Three shots. Two lions." They embroidered and embellished it as they sang it, one clear voice falling in after the other: "Three good shots, two big strong bad kali lions." And then they all joined into an intoxicated refrain: "A.B.C.D.",—because they came straight from the school, and had their heads filled with wisdom.

In a short time a great number of people came to the spot, the laborers from the mill, the squatters of the near manyattas, and my houseboys, carrying hurricane-lamps. They stood round the lions and talked about them, then Kanuthia and the Sice, who had brought knives, set to skin them. It was the skin of one of these lions that, later, I gave to the Indian High Priest. Pooran Singh himself appeared on the stage, in a negligée which made him look unbelievably slight, his melliferous Indian smile shone in the midst of his thick black heard, he stuttered with delight when he spoke. He was anxious to procure for himself the fat of the lions, that with his people is held in high esteem as a medicine,—from the pantomime by which he expressed himself to me, I believe against rheumatism and impotence. With all this the coffee-field became very lively, the rain stopped, the moon shone down on them all.

We went back to the house and Juma brought and opened our bottle. We were too wet, and too dirty with mud and blood to sit down to it, but stood up before a flaming fire in the dining room and drank our live, singing wine up quickly. We did not speak one word. In our hunt we had been a unity and we had nothing to say to one another.

Our friends got a good deal of entertainment out of our adventure. Old Mr. Bulpett when next we came in to a dance at the Club would not speak to us the whole evening.

# PREDILECTIONS

Le Anne Schreiber

I EAT MEAT. I carry a leather handbag. I am not above reproach. I fish. I wouldn't dream of hunting. I catch and release trout. I catch and eat bass. I can be accused of inconsistency. Is the inconsistency moral, logical, sentimental? To whom do I have to answer?

No matter what choices I make, I am complicit. If I forswear meat and leather, shouldn't I also forswear bread and cotton? The clearing of forest and plains to cultivate what feeds, clothes and shelters me kills as certainly and perhaps more cruelly than bullets. Is slow death by destruction of habitat more humane than a quick kill by bullet? Where between the blithe swatting of a mosquito and the tender release of a trout do I draw the line? Is there a weak link in the food chain that separates the sacrificial from the sacrosanct?

These questions remained abstract, by which I mean they caused little loss of sleep, as long as I lived an urban existence. But it has been fifteen years now that I have lived in a rural patch of upstate New York where I consort far more regularly with critters than humans. Deer, coyotes, foxes, skunks, raccoons, beaver, muskrats, trout, bass, ducks, geese, hawks, owls, the occasional osprey or eagle—they are, in effect, my neighbors, and I feel the need for a commandment to guide my behavior toward them.

Playing favorites, as I have done with trout and bass, is an inadequate ethic, in part because the favoritism is based on sentiments that keep shifting. When I lived in a hamlet whose contours were defined by the stream that ran through it, I developed a personal history with particular tout, like the trout who jumped every evening at dusk under the farthest tip of the maple branch that reached to the middle of the stream where it ran behind Betty's barn. I caught and released him many times over several years, and when I finally caught another, smaller fish in his place, I knew he had come to a bad end, which I regretted.

Because I enjoyed walking in streams more than rowing across lakes, I cultivated no comparable friendships among bass. Bass were dinner, until I built a house on a lake and bought a kayak. Now I know individual bass, like the one who leaps at dusk every day in the opening among the lily pads to the left of the dock. Kayaks are lousy to fish from, but they are a great perch for fish watching. I visit nests, wondering not how the blue gills make such perfect circles in the silt, but how they are able to position dozens of such circles so they are exactly equidistant from one another in all directions, as if they had stolen the template from which furnace filters are made.

Since moving to the lake, I fish less and less, but not out of sentiment for the little ones. I could catch and release bass or blue gills, and I still occasionally do, but now that I have secured myself an orchestra seat on water, I find that I derive more enjoyment from observing than angling, just as I always took more pleasure in tracking than shooting. Catching a peek is what I'm after. I resent the intrusions of other fishermen because they might catch the bass who leaps so foolhardily at dusk, giving definition to my day.

This is not a moral stance. I would sacrifice a bass any day to see the show-stopping ostentation of an osprey's wing-flared, talons-first plunge, the splash and flap of his catching without a thought of release. I have even lurked in my kayak under an overhanging branch while the osprey above is ripping flesh from his prey. There's no fish blood on my hands, but I've had it splattered from above onto my hair while I was waiting for the thrilling moment, sure to come, when the osprey fixes his yellow eyes on my green ones and rivets me in exactly the place I want to be.

I suppose I could exalt my preference for rarer displays over more common ones, for osprey plunges over bass leaps, into an ethic based on the relative endangerment of species, but the distinction would be morally specious. My preferences are entirely self-serving, based on a species' capacity to satisfy my appetites. That those appetites are born of aesthetic impulse or intellectual curiosity rather than hunger or blood lust is, morally speaking, beside the point. Some good might follow from my preferences, if I widely propagandized them, but they don't secure my footing on any moral high ground.

A predilection for the open-endedness of observation over the closure of a kill renders some questions moot, but it doesn't serve as a guide for behavior when a species, rare or common, presents itself not as spectacle but nuisance. These days I find that it's not hunting or fishing that poses the hard questions. It's homeowning. The deer who leaves tracks for me to follow on the hillside that flanks the opposite shore is entertainment; the deer who eats my shrubbery is aggravation. The coyotes who yip and howl on clear moonlit nights are a welcome note in the soundtrack of country living; the coyote who mauled my neighbor's cat is an object of fear. The beaver who cruises the lake at dusk, crossing his wake with mine as I swim on summer evenings, is a compatriot; the beaver whose dam raises the water level of the lake can be either friend or foe.

Last summer, when the entire east coast was in the grip of what weather pundits were calling the drought of the century, the lake stayed, to my pleasant surprise, at its optimally convenient level—high enough to discourage weediness, not so high that it threatened to flood my new house, built of necessity on land too low for comfort. It was my first summer on the lake, and I attributed that good fortune to the apparently undiminished strength of the springs that feed the lake. Then came September and the heavy rains of Hurricane Floyd. The water level rose 8 inches, but did not in due course subside. A few more inches and the elaborate system of DEC-approved underground drains that siphon groundwater away from my house would flow backwards, welcoming the lake into my home.

No longer complacent about the cause of unfluctuating water levels, I investigated, i.e., I donned waders and slogged through a marsh of head high reeds at the lake's southern end until I found the source of the problem—a beaver dam constructed across a narrowing, about 6 feet wide, where marsh water funnels into an outlet creek flanked by well-chomped woods. The dam, which presumably had kept the lake conveniently high during the summer drought, was now keeping it inconveniently high during an unseasonable wet fall. Using a variety of large pointed sticks borrowed from the top of the adjacent beaver hutch, I poked a large enough breach in the mud-and-twig dam to send the water coursing at a good clip through the creek bed toward the Roe Jan and on to the Hudson, perhaps even to the Atlantic, which seemed a good safe distance away from my house. It was just like pulling the stopper from a bath-tub drain, only muddier and a lot more gratifying.

The next day, when the lake level had dropped only 2 inches, I returned to find the beavers had rebuilt. I dismantled the dam again, this time creating a larger breach that I hoped would in-crease both the volume of released water and the beavers' rebuild-ing time. This back and forth of building and breaching went on between us for two months, its pace determined by the frequency and intensity of rains last fall. The pace never slackened to less than twice a week, and for certain stretches it was a daily battle, in-creasingly tedious and time-consuming. I learned that the beavers, whom I never saw, did most of their rebuilding at night, so it be-hooved me to do my part earlier in the day to reap maximal release time. They learned to build smaller satellite dams down-stream to slow the release of water from my larger and deeper breaches.

I hacked an overland route through the woods to spare myself marshy slogs, and I started taking implements with me, a hoe one day, a rake the next. They countered by upping the sophistication of their engineering. They scavenged a partial roll of rusty chicken wire someone had discarded in the woods and used it as dam infra-structure. They buttressed the dam by crafting branches into long sticks with one forked end and one pointed end; the forked end was placed perpendicular to the dam and the pointy end was jammed deep into either the creek bed or the banks downstream.

It was taking me at least two hours a day to create a decent breach in the main and satellite dams; add another half-hour for travel time to and from the dam, not to mention shower and laun-dry time to clean the muck off me and my clothes. This was not fun any more. I considered hiring a trapper.

The considerations were serious. I knew local trapping practices were not critter-friendly. Even if I made a trapper promise to relocate rather than kill the beavers, I knew from my home-building experience that getting a subcontractor's word did not insure getting his deed. But the stakes were high for me as well. The physical integrity of my only home was at risk. The beavers could build elsewhere. In fact, there were already two perfectly fine hutches right on the lake, where they posed no threat because naturally deep water near the rocky bank made dam building unnecessary. I would be happy to share habitat with the beavers if they would only use those. On the other hand, perhaps they had abandoned those hutches in response to my arrival. I was the interloper after all. They had been here first.

That last factor—that they had been here first—weighed heavily on me, because I was not just a homeowner, I was a homebuilder. When you build on land that has never been built on before in living or recorded history, there can be no innocence in the act. You are not disturbing further an already disturbed habitat; you are doing the dirty deed of bending nature to your will, and you reap the consequences, good or ill. If you aren't blind, you see your impact, and you are, for the most part, your own judge and jury in weighing the guilt/cost/benefit.

When the judge and jury weighed in, the verdict was this: I would pursue a course of proportionate force. That meant maintaining the status quo of evenly matched adversaries: one woman, her hoe and hip boots vs. an undetermined number of beavers, their sharp teeth and agile paws. Any disproportion in industry was my problem to remedy. If I wanted to live on a lake and enjoy the entertaining company of critters, I had to accept whatever labor intensiveness that entailed. Another way of putting it: if they threatened my home, I could threaten theirs. I couldn't otherwise endanger them

Strangely enough, while I was coming to this conclusion, the beavers made an accommodation of their own. The last time they reconstructed the dam, they left a small breach top-center, just enough to let the water level maintain an equilibrium that is acceptable to me and presumably to them as well. By December ice had formed on the marsh, and they seem to have taken the winter off. Spring thaws may renew the conflict, but I feel equipped with something closer to principle than predilection to guide my behavior, and not only toward the beavers. When the skunk returns to eat the grubs in my lawn, I can return his spray with my best shot from the hose, but if I throw rocks at him, as I have done in the past, my aim has to be off. If a coyote comes for my cat, my aim will be true.

The commandment-in-progress will probably not cover all situations, and it doesn't begin to answer the questions about my complicity in what others do in the name of providing my food and shelter. It's not a categorical, just a personal imperative, one that allows me to act without waiting for light from on high about the imponderables.

There's another personal imperative that underlies this one. I have seen the moment of death, the last pulse, respiration, twitch. The spider's legs shriveled. The fish black and still. The face blanched. Always, it shocks, the shock so curiously the same however different the loss. Not everyone feels this way. They say the moment is natural, meant to be, and I know that's often true, but I also know I am not meant to deliver that moment. This stance is not moral, logical, sentimental. It's visceral.

# My War on *Marmota Monax*

## Louise Jones

I always thought that I could kill to protect my children, but in no other circumstances, although my son would be dubious. When he was about ten, we were below decks in a small boat and I saw him examining something on the wall. "What is it?" I asked. "A bat, Mom, and it's real neat!" Terrified of bats, I blindly bolted up the companionway. A few minutes later my son followed calmly and joked, "Some mother—you didn't even try to protect me—just ran."

I never was put in the position where I had to kill for my children, but there was a time when I did kill to protect my vegetable garden, which to me was like a third child: it needed nurturing, care, watchfulness, persistence, even love. It was also very important to me, and still is, as a source of food for the family. We kill to eat—whether it's wild game or a chicken or a flounder—and I killed not to provide the food but to prevent a predatory woodchuck from taking it.

Our garden was close to the house, enclosed by a rather flimsy wood and wire fence, a totally inadequate three feet high. A dilapidated tool shed stood in the back of the yard, set into a hill that hosted woodchuck families every summer. They lived in the hillside with many escape holes, one of which went right through a rotten portion of the tool shed floor. The woodchuck, *Marmota monax,* is a strict vegetarian. Plump, sassy animals, coated with sleek dark brown hair, they afforded, as they scooted around the yard, great excitement for our dogs and cats. With acres of cultivated lawn, shrubs, and flowers, as well as weeds and woodlands on their menu, the woodchucks (some call them groundhogs) preferred the lettuce, beans, peas, and parsley in my garden. Ours was not the only one. All my gardening friends complained about woodchuck depredation. The critters could be seen chowing down along every roadside. As angry as I was at their attacks on my plants, I would swerve my car to avoid hitting them as they waddled across the roads. The large number of dead woodchucks along the roads proved that many people didn't bother, and the sight both pleased me that there was one less woodchuck in the neighborhood and saddened me that a basically innocent creature had been hit by a car. My daughter, tenderhearted regarding cuddly-looking creatures, covered her eyes and groaned whenever we passed road kill.

Of course, when you garden in the suburbs, woodchucks are not the only problem. Our house was about an hour north of New York City, at the edge of a thousand wooded acres from which deer would venture into the garden, clearing the fence effortlessly. In the winter, when ice and snow covered the shrubs and weeds they usually ate, they also made the rounds of the foundation plantings against the house. There were so many raccoons that we gave up trying to grow sweet corn. In a manner seemingly traditional to them, the raccoons would sample each ear of ripe corn the night before we were planning to pick it. Rabbits were as common as lady bugs.

We tried an array of organic methods to discourage the animals: bloodmeal sprinkled around the perimeter of the garden and human hair (the woman who cut my hair saved her sweepings for me) stuffed into little bags made from old pantyhose and hung on the fence, pea supports, and corn stalks. Supposedly the odor of blood and hair would repel animals; it did until the first rain or even heavy dew. We sprayed the vegetables with a homemade hot pepper and garlic spray that my son called Mom's Deadly Gazpacho, which killed aphids and other insects but didn't deter the four-footed pests. We tried leaving our dog tied up in the garden overnight, but his barking kept us awake. For a couple of weeks we placed a portable radio, set at an all night talk show, in the middle of the corn patch to scare away the raccoons, but they adapted to the voices even though we changed talk shows every few nights. We decided against electric fencing, fearing injury to children and pets.

One lovely late afternoon of a lush summer I entered my garden to find a woodchuck, with the typical Roman nose and haughty demeanor, on her hind legs selecting green beans. As I opened the gate in the fence, the animal idly turned her head toward me with a look that said "Wait your turn," apparently unsure whether she wanted Tendercrop bush beans or Kentucky Wonder pole beans for her dinner. She didn't trundle off until I clapped my hands and yelled, and then not very quickly. She was a large female who, with her five adorable pups, had frequently gamboled over the lawn during the early summer. I could empathize with a nursing mama's need to keep up her strength, and I hadn't begrudged her the row of early lettuce she'd mowed down nor the lower-growing peas she'd plucked. But by the time the beans were at their succulent best, her babies were more than six weeks old and on their own.

To add to my outrage, that same month a self-congratulatory letter had appeared in the gardening section of the New York Times. The kindly writer, who lived in the southern part of the county, described her foolproof method for ridding her garden of woodchucks. She caught them in Hav-A-Heart traps and drove them to the "northern" part of the county where she released them near the "woods."

"That's us," I shouted apoplectically to my husband. "They're sending their woodchucks to summer camp in our yard!" We lived in an old house between the road and the woods, and people had left kittens at our doorstep, so why not woodchucks?

I had to take action to protect my vegetables. A kitchen window overlooked the space between the tool shed and the garden fence. My husband raised the screen and for two days he and our son took turns, whenever feasible, staking out the lawn with a lever-action Marlin .22 rifle. Fortunately for peace in the family, our daughter was out of town visiting a friend. But the woodchuck evaded us. The third afternoon, while my husband was away and my son was taking a shower, I glanced out the kitchen window and saw Ms. Woodchuck hustling toward the garden.

When I was a teenager my father had an air pistol and we used to sit on the porch shooting at paper targets. I developed pretty good aim, but never thought of myself as a shooter. The only animal I'd ever shot was from a duck blind, a big, slow-flying mallard, and the thrill at seeing it ker-splash into the water was quickly cancelled out by a feeling of remorse for having killed it.

But this was war. I instinctively grabbed the rifle and swung it at the fat woodchuck that was actually leaping for the fence as I aimed and pulled the trigger. BAM! She fell to the ground. My son clattered down the stairs, looked out the window, and shouted "Mom! You hit it! Great!" There was an immediate knot in my stomach. I couldn't look at the dead animal and asked my son to check it out and bury the body. He said afterward that I'd shot her clean through the neck and she must have died instantly.

We now live in Vermont and our vegetable garden is surrounded by a sturdy fence more than six feet high, the wire buried a foot or so underground to prevent burrowers—"Stalag Jones" my husband calls it. That, and a Jack Russell Terrier who yips when she hears a leaf fall outside much less an animal rustling, are adequate protection.

Every gardener is constantly battling animal and insect pests. We have very little compunction about killing bugs, but we're reluctant to kill warm-blooded, four-legged trespassers, especially those that suckle their young. It may be out of sentimentality or a Jungian identification with or fear of them. I've seen people swat mosquitoes with abandon, then become outraged at the shooting of a rabbit. On the other hand, humans are adept at altering their priorities. A city friend who was rabidly anti-hunting for years asked my husband if he'd shoot the deer who were eating the lovely dogwoods and azaleas on her newly-purchased country property.

Although it was more than 25 years ago, I retain a feeling of guilt, not for the way I killed the woodchuck, because I dropped her cleanly with the first shot, but that I resorted to killing. I was enraged and killed her to protect my vegetables, as I know I would kill to protect my children, whether from a predatory bear or a mountain lion or from a human intruder. Now I would like to think that if our substantial fence doesn't keep the woodchucks out, I'm willing to share. But there's the problem: animals don't share, they take it all. If you want a vegetable garden, and all other measures fail, you have to be prepared to kill. I'm very glad we have the fence so that I haven't had to shoot any more woodchucks, but just as I use my deadly gazpacho to get rid of insect pests, I would pick up the rifle again against another woodchuck invasion. It would be that or give up the garden.

Right now the war is over: One down, six zillion woodchucks left standing.

# Part Seven

*We had the morning to hunt. Now it was almost noon and we were work-*
*ing our way back to the car, my father's game pockets, as always, bulging,*
*mine, as always, empty, when, emerging from a woods into a clearing, the*
*two dogs simultaneously set. Tails stiff and straight out behind them,*
*heads high, they seemed to be holding the birds transfixed by their steady*
*stare. When I kicked, three birds flushed, two one way, one another. So*
*rapid were my father's two shots that they seemed one, and to each a bird,*
*in a burst of feathers, fell. I in my pottering way was following the lone*
*bird, when my father swiveled, found it, and fired. He scored a clean miss.*
*I fired, and in a third burst of feathers on the air, that bird fell. I acted as*
*though I was used to doing it daily. So did my father, and he was offhand*
*in his congratulations to me. But he was almost visibly puffed with pride.*
*That he himself had missed the bird doubled his pleasure. Forgotten were*
*the uncountable number of quail he had brought down in his time when-*
*ever he told the story of that one of mine. Before long he was omitting to*
*mention the two he had gotten on that rise before I killed the one he had*
*shot at and missed.*

—William Humphrey
"The Guns of Boyhood," from *Open Season* (1986)

# Praise God for the Blood of the Bull

## Beryl Markham

ARAB MAINA CLASPED the gourd of blood and curdled milk in both hands and looked toward the sun. He chanted in a low voice:

"Praise God for the blood of the bull which brings strength to our loins, and for the milk of the cow which gives warmth to the breasts of our lovers."

He drank deeply of the gourd then, let his belch roll upward from his belly and resound against the morning silence. It was a silence that we who stood there preserved until Arab Maina had finished, because this was religion; it was the ritual that came before the hunt. It was the Nandi custom.

"Praise God for the blood of the bull," we said, and stood before the singiri, and waited.

Jebbta had brought the gourds for Arab Maina, for Arab Kosky, and for me. But she looked only at me.

"The heat of a Murani is like unto stone," she whispered, "and his limbs have the speed of an antelope. Where do you find the strength and the daring to hunt with them, my sister?"

We were as young as each other, Jebbta and I, but she was a Nandi, and if the men of the Nandi were like unto stone, their women were like unto leaves of grass. They were shy and they were feminine and they did the things that women are meant to do, and they never hunted.

I looked down at the ankle-length skins Jebbta wore, which rustled like taffeta when she moved, and she looked at my khaki shorts and lanky, naked legs.

"Your body is like mine," she said; "it is the same and it is no stronger." She turned, avoiding the men with her eyes, because that too was law, and went quickly away tittering like a small bird.

"The blood of the bull . . ." said Arab Maina.

"We are ready." Arab Kosky drew his sword from its scabbard and tested its blade. The scabbard was of leather, dyed red, and it hung on a beaded belt that encircled narrow and supple hips. He tested the blade and put it back into the red scabbard.

"By the sacred womb of my mother, we will kill the wild boar today!"

He moved forward behind Arab Maina with his broad shield and his straight spear, and I followed Arab Kosky with my own spear that was still new and very clean, and lighter than theirs. Behind me came Buller with no spear and no shield, but with the heart of a hunter and jaws that were weapons enough. There were the other dogs, but there was no dog like Buller.

We left the singiri with the first light of the sun warming the roofs of the huts, with cattle, goats, and sheep moving along the trails that led to open pastures—fat cattle, pampered cattle, attended as always by the young, uncircumcised boys.

There were cows, steers, and heifers—liquid brown eyes, wet, friendly nostrils, slobbery mouths that covered our legs with sticky fluid as Arab Maina pushed the stupid heads aside with his shield.

There were the pungent stench of goat's urine and a hot, comforting odor seeping through the hides of the cattle, and light on the long muscles of Arab Maina and Arab Kosky.

There was the whole of the day ahead—and the world to hunt in.

His little ritual forgotten now, Arab Maina was no longer stern. He laughed when Arab Kosky or I slipped in the cattle dung that littered our path, and shook his spear at a big black bull busy tearing up the earth with his hooves. "Take care of your people and dare not insult me with a barren cow this year!"

But, for the most part, we ran silently in single file skirting the edge of the dense Mau Forest, wheeling north to descend into the Rongai Valley, its bottom a thousand feet below us.

Eight weeks had passed since the end of the heavy rains and the grass in the valley had already reached the height of a man's knee. The ears had begun to ripen in patches. Looking down upon it, the whole was like a broad counterpane dyed in rust and yellow and golden brown.

We filed along our path, almost invisible now, through the fresh-smelling leleshwa bush, avoiding with quick turns and careful leaps the stinging nettle and the shrubs that were armed with thorns. Buller ran at my heels with the native dogs spread fanwise behind.

Halfway down the slope of the valley a bevy of partridges rose from the grass and wheeled noisily into the sky. Arab Maina lifted his spear almost imperceptibly; Arab Kosky's long muscles were suddenly rigid. Watching him, I froze in my tracks and held my breath. It was the natural reaction of all hunters—that moment of listening after any alarm.

But there was nothing. The spear of Arab Maina dipped gently, the long muscles of Arab Kosky sprang again to life, Buller flicked his stubby tail, and we were off again, one behind another, with the warm sunlight weaving a pattern of our shadows in the thicket.

The heat of the valley rose to meet us. Singing cicadas, butterflies like flowers before a wind fluttered against our bodies or hovered over the low bush. Only small things that were safe in the daylight moved.

We had run another mile before the cold nose of Buller nudged against my leg and the dog slipped quickly past me, past the two Murani, to plant himself, alert and motionless, in the center of our path.

"Stop." I whispered the word, putting my hand on Arab Kosky's shoulder. "Buller has scented something."

"I believe you are right, Lakweit!" With a wave of his hand Arab Kosky ordered the pack of native dogs to crouch. In that they were well trained. They pressed their lean bodies on the ground, cocked their ears, but scarcely seemed to breathe.

Arab Maina, sensing the need for free action, began laying down his shield. The fingers of his left hand still touched the worn leather of its handle, his legs were still bent at the knee, when a male reed-buck bounded high into the air more than fifty yards away.

I saw Arab Kosky's body bend like a bow and watched his spear fly to his shoulder, but he was too late. The spear of Arab Maina flashed in a quick arc of silver light and the reed-buck fell with the hard point sunk deep under his heart. Not even his first frantic bound had been completed before Arab Maina's arm had brought him down.

"Karara-ni! The hand of our leader is swifter than the flight of an arrow and stronger than the stroke of a leopard." Heaping praise on Arab Maina, Arab Kosky ran toward the fallen reed-buck, the sword from his red leather sheath drawn for the kill.

I looked at Arab Maina's slender arms with their even, flat muscles and saw no visible sign of such immense strength. Arab Maina, like Arab Kosky, was tall and lithe as a young bamboo, and his skin glowed like an ember under a whisper of wind. His face was young and hard, but there was soft humor in it. There was love of life in it—love for the hunt, love for the sureness of his strength, love for the beauty and usefulness of his spear.

The spear was made of pliant steel tempered and forged by the metallist of his own tribe. But it was also more than that.

To each Murani his spear is a symbol of his manhood, and as much a part of himself as the sinews of his body. His spear is a manifestation of his faith; without it he can achieve nothing—no land, no cattle, no wives. Not even honor can be his until that day comes, after his circumcision, when he stands before the gathered members of his tribe—men and women of all ages, from manyattas as scattered as the seeds of wild grass—and swears allegiance to them and to their common heritage.

He takes the spear from the hands of the ol-oiboni and holds it, as he will always hold it while there is strength in his arms and no cloud of age before his eyes. It is the emblem of his blood and his breeding, and possessing it, he is suddenly a man.

Possessing it, it is never afterward beyond his reach.

Arab Maina placed his left foot on the reed-buck and carefully drew out his spear.

"I do not know, it may have struck a bone," he said.

He ran bloody fingers along the sharp edges of the weapon and let a little smile twist his lips. "By the will of God, the metal is not chipped! My spear is unhurt." He stooped to pluck a handful of grass and wiped the blood from the bright, warm steel.

Arab Kosky and I had already begun to skin the animal, using our "bushman's friends." There was not much time to waste, because our real hunt for the wild boar had not yet begun. But still the meat of the reed-buck would provide food for the dogs.

"The sun has hit the valley," said Arab Maina; "if we do not hurry the pigs will have gone in all directions like rolling weeds in a wind."

Arab Kosky buried his fingers along the walls of the reed-buck's stomach, tearing it from the animal's frame.

"Hold this, Lakwani," he said, 'and help me separate the intestines for the dogs."

I took the slippery, jelly-like stomach in my hands and held it while I kneeled over the reed-buck.

"Maina, I still don't know how you managed to throw in time from the position you were in!"

Arab Kosky smiled.

"He is a Murani, Lakwani—and a Murani must always throw in time. Otherwise, some day a dangerous animal might charge swifter than the spear. Then, instead of mourning his death, our girls would laugh and say he should have stayed at home with the old men!"

Arab Maina leaned down and cut a chunk of meat from the cleanly skinned buck. He handed it to me for Buller. The rest, he and Arab Kosky left to the native mongrels.

Buller trotted a short distance away from the kill, dropped his reward in a little pool of shade, and regarded his snarling cousins with exquisite disdain. In the language that he spoke, and only I understood, he said quite clearly (with just a tinge of Swahili accent), "By the noble ancestry of my bull terrier father, those animals behave like the wild dog!"

"And now," said Arab Maina, moving away from the carnage, "we must make ready for the hunt."

The two Murani wore ochre-colored shukas, each falling loosely from a single knot on the left shoulder, and each looking somewhat like a scanty Roman toga. They untied the knots now, wrapped the shukas prudently around their waists, and stood in the sun, the muscles in their backs rippling under their oiled skins like fretted water over a stony bed.

"Who can move freely with clothes on his body?" Arab Kosky said as he helped Arab Maina with the leather thong that bound his braided headdress in place. "Who has seen the antelope run with rags upon his back to hinder his speed!"

"Who indeed?" said Arab Maina, smiling. "I think sometimes you babble like a demented goat, Kosky. The sun is high and the valley still lies below us—and you speak to Lakwani of antelope wearing shukas! Take up your spears, my friends, and let us go."

Single file again, with Arab Maina in the lead, then Arab Kosky, then myself, and Buller just behind, we ran on down into the valley.

There were no clouds and the sun stared down on the plain making heat waves rise from it like flames without color.

The Equator runs close to the Rongai Valley, and, even at so high an altitude as this we hunted in, the belly of the earth was hot as live ash under our feet. Except for an occasional gust of fretful wind that flattened the high, corn-like grass, nothing uttered—nothing in the valley stirred. The chirrup-like drone of grasshoppers was dead, birds left the sky unmarked. The sun reigned and there were no aspirants to his place.

We stopped by the red salt-lick that cropped out of the ground in the path of our trail. I did not remember a time when the salt-lick was as deserted as this. Always before it had been crowded with grantii, impala, kongoni, eland, water-buck, and a dozen kinds of smaller animals. But it was empty today. It was like a marketplace whose flow and bustle of life you had witnessed ninety-nine times, but, on your hundredth visit, was vacant and still without even an urchin to tell you why.

I put my hand on Arab Maina's arm. "What are you thinking, Maina? Why is there no game today?"

"Be quiet, Lakweit, and do not move."

I dropped the butt of my spear on the earth and watched the two Murani stand still as trees, their nostrils distended, their ears alert to all things. Arab Kosky's hand was tight on his spear like the claw of an eagle clasping a branch.

"It is an odd sign," murmured Arab Maina, "when the salt-lick is without company!"

I had forgotten Buller, but the dog had not forgotten us. He had not forgotten that, with all the knowledge of the two Murani, he still knew better about such things. He thrust his body roughly between Arab Maina and myself, holding his black wet nose close to the ground. And the hairs along his spine stiffened. His hackles rose and he trembled.

We might have spoken, but we didn't. In his way Buller was more eloquent. Without a sound, he said, as clearly as it could be said—"Lion."

"Do not move, Lakweit." Arab Kosky stepped closer to me.

"Steady, Buller," I whispered to the dog, trying to soothe his rising belligerence.

Our eyes followed the direction of Arab Maina's eyes. He was staring into a small grass-curtained donga a few yards from the edge of the salt-lick.

The lion that stood in the donga was not intimidated by Arab Maina's stare. He was not concerned with our number. He swung his tail in easy arcs, stared back through the wispy grass, and his manner said, "I am within my rights. If you seek a battle, what are we waiting for?"

He moved slowly forward, increasing the momentum of his tail, flaunting his thick black mane.

"Ach! This is bad! He is angry—he wants to attack!" Arab Maina spoke in an undertone.

No animal, however fast, has greater speed than a charging lion over a distance of a few yards. It is a speed faster than thought—faster always than escape.

Under my restraining hand I felt the muscles of Buller knot and relax, in a surging flow of mounting fury. Buller's mind had reached its blind spot. Uncontrolled, he would throw himself in gallant suicide straight at the lion. I dug my fingers into the dog's coat and held tight.

Arab Maina's appearance was transformed. His face had taken on a sullen, arrogant expression, his square, bold jaw jutted forward. His eyes dimmed almost dreamily and sank behind high, shiny cheekbones. I watched the muscles on his neck swell like those on the neck of an angry snake, and saw flecks of white froth appear in the corners of his mouth. Passive and rigid he stared back at the lion.

He raised his shield at last, as if to make sure it was still in his hand, and let his spear arm drop to his side to preserve all of its power for whatever might come.

He knew that if the lion attacked, his own skill and Arab Kosky's would, in the end, prove sufficient—but not before at least one of us had been killed or badly mauled. Arab Maina was more than a Murani; he was a leader of Murani, and as such he must be able to think as well as to fight. He must be capable of strategy.

Watching him still, as he in turn watched the lion, I knew that he had a plan of action.

"Observe his eyes," he said; "he thinks very hard of many things. He believes that we also think of those same things. We must show him that we are fearless as he himself is fearless, but that his desires are not our desires. We must walk straight past him firmly and with courage, and we must shame his anger by laughter and loud talk."

Arab Kosky's brow was dotted with small bubbles of sweat. A slight flicker of a smile crept over his face.

"Yes, true enough! The lion thinks of many things. I too think of many things, and so does Lakweit. But your plan is a good one. We will try it."

Arab Maina lifted his head a little higher, turning it only enough to keep the lion within the scope of his vision. He placed one sinewy leg in front of the other, and stiffly, like a man walking the trunk of a tree that bridges a chasm, he began to move. One after another, we followed. My hand still lay upon Buller's neck, but Arab Kosky let the dog and me slip past him to walk between the two Murani.

"Stay close to me, Lakweit"—Arab Maina's voice was anxious. "I fear for you when it is not possible to see you."

Arab Kosky burst suddenly into forced laughter.

"There is a tale about a rhino who needed a needle to do her husband's sewing . . ." he began.

"So she borrowed one from the porcupine . . ." said Arab Kosky.

"And swallowed it," I contributed. "I have heard that tale before, Kosky!"

The Murani laughed louder. "But perhaps our friend the lion has not. Look at him. He is listening!"

"But not laughing," said Arab Maina. "He moves as we move. He comes closer!"

The lion had stalked out of the donga. Now, as we walked, we could see that he guarded the slain body of a large kongoni. Smears of blood were fresh on his forelegs, his jowls, and his chest. He was a lone hunter—an individualist—a solitary marauder. His tail had stopped swinging. His great head turned exactly in ratio to the speed of our stride. The full force of the lion-smell, meaty, pungent, almost indescribable, struck against our nostrils.

"Having swallowed the needle . . ." said Arab Kosky.

"Silence—he attacks!"

I do not know who moved with greater speed—Arab Maina or the lion. I believe it must have been Arab Maina. I think the Murani anticipated the charge even before the lion moved, and because of that, it was a battle of wills instead of weapons.

The lion rushed from the fringe of the donga like a rock from a catapult. He stopped like the same rock striking the walls of a battlement.

Arab Maina was down on his left knee. Beside him was Arab Kosky. Each man, with his shield, his spear, and his body, was a fighting machine no longer human, but only motionless and precise and coldly ready. Buller and I crouched behind them, my own spear as ready as I could make it in hands that were less hot from the sun than from excitement and the pounding of my heart.

"Steady, Buller."

"Do not move, Lakweit."

The lion had stopped. He stood a few strides from Arab Maina's buffalo-hide shield, stared into Arab Maina's eyes challenging him over the top of it, and swung his tail like the weight of a clock. At that moment I think the ants in the grass paused in their work.

And then Arab Maina stood up.

I do not know how he knew that that particular instant was the right instant or how he knew that the lion would accept a truce. It may have been accomplished by the sheer arrogance of Arab Maina's decision to lower his shield, even if slightly, and to rise, no longer warlike, and to beckon us on with superb and sudden indifference. But however it was, the lion never moved.

We left him slicing the tall grass with his heavy tail, the blood of the kongoni drying on his coat. He was thinking many things.

And I was disappointed. Long after we had continued our trot toward the place where we knew there would be warthog, I thought how wonderful it would have been if the lion had attacked and I had been able to use my spear on him while he clawed at the shields of the two Murani, and how later they might have said, "If it hadn't been for you, Lakweit! . . ."

But then, I was very young.

We ran until we reached the Molo River.

The river took its life from the Mau Escarpment and twisted down into the valley and gave life, in turn, to mimosa trees with crowns as broad as clouds, and long creepers and liana that strangled the sunlight and left the riverbank soothing and dark.

The earth on the bank was damp and pitted with footprints of the game that followed a web-work of thin trails to drink at dawn, leaving the racy smell of their droppings and their bodies in the air. The river forest was narrow and cool and vibrant with the songs of multi-colored birds, and clotted with bright flowers that scorned the sun.

We laid down our weapons and rested under the trees and drank the chilled water, making cups with our hands.

Arab Maina lifted his face from the edge of the river and smiled gently. "My mouth was like unto ashes, Lakweit," he said, "but truly this water is even sweeter than Jebbta's carefully brewed tembo!"

"It is sweeter," said Arab Kosky, "and at this moment it is more welcome. I promise you, my stomach had turned almost sour with thirst!"

Looking at me, Arab Maina laughed.

"Sour with thirst, he says, Lakweit! Sour, I think, with the sight of the lion at the salt-lick. Courage lives in a man's stomach, but there are times when it is not at home—and then the stomach is sour!"

Arab Kosky stretched his lithe, straight limbs on the tangled grass and smiled, showing teeth white as sun-cured bone. "Talk lives in a man's head," he answered, "but sometimes it is very lonely because in the heads of some men there is nothing to keep it company—and so talk goes out through the lips."

I laughed with both of them and pressed my shoulders comfortably against the tree I leaned upon and looked through a chink in the ceiling of the forest at a vulture flying low.

"Maina, you know, I hate those birds. Their wings are separated like a lot of small snakes."

"As you say, Lakwani, they are creatures of evil omen—messengers of the dead. Too cowardly to slay for themselves, they are satisfied with the stinking flesh from another man's kill." Arab Maina spat, as if to clean his mouth after talking of unpleasant things.

Buller and the native dogs had gone into the river and wallowed in the cool black muck along its banks. Buller returned now, sleek with slime, dripping and happy. He waited until he had the two Murani and me easily within range and then shook himself with a kind of devilish impudence and stood wagging his stump tail as we wiped water and mud from our faces.

"It is his way of making a joke," said Arab Kosky, looking at his spattered shuka.

"It is also his way of telling us to move," said Arab Maina. "The hunter who lies on his back in the forest has little food and no sport. We have spent much time today at other things, but the warthog still waits."

"What you say is true." Arab Kosky rose from the grass. "The warthog still waits, and who is so without manners as to keep another waiting? Surely Buller is not. We must take his advice and go."

We went up the riverbank, falling into single file again, and threaded our way through a labyrinth of silver-gray boulders and rust-red anthills, shaped variously like witches caps or like the figures of kneeling giants or like trees without branches. Some of the anthills were enormous, higher than the huts we lived in, and some were no higher than our knees. They were scattered everywhere.

"Seek 'em out, Buller!"

But the dog needed no urging from me. He knew warthog country when he saw it and he knew what to do about it. He rushed on ahead followed by the native mongrels running in a little storm of their own dust.

I know animals more gallant than the African warthog, but none more courageous. He is the peasant of the plains—the drab and dowdy digger in the earth. He is the uncomely but intrepid defender of family, home, and bourgeois convention, and he will fight anything of any size that intrudes upon his smug existence. Even his weapons are plebeian—curved tusks, sharp, deadly, but not beautiful, used inelegantly for rooting as well as for fighting.

He stands higher than a domestic pig when he is full grown, and his hide is dust-colored and tough and clothed in bristles. His eyes are small and lightless and capable of but one expression—suspicion. What he does not understand, he suspects, and what he suspects, he fights. He can leap into the air and gut a horse while its rider still ponders a strategy of attack, and his speed in emerging from his hole to demonstrate the advantage of surprise is almost phenomenal.

He is not lacking in guile. He enters his snug little den (which is borrowed, not to say commandeered, from its builder, the ant-bear) tail foremost so that he is never caught off guard. While he lies thus in wait for the curiosity or indiscretion of his enemy to bring him within range, he uses his snout to pile a heap of fine dust inside the hole. The dust serves as a smoke screen, bursting into a great, enshrouding billow the moment the warthog emerges to battle. He understands the tactical retreat, but is incapable of surrender, and if a dog is less than a veteran, or a man no more than an intrepid novice, not the only blood spilled will be the warthog's.

These facts were always in my mind when Buller hunted with us, as he always did. But there was never any question of leaving him. It would have been like preventing a born soldier from marching with his regiment or like denying a champion fighter the right to compete in the ring on the grounds that he might be hurt. So Buller always came, and often I worried.

He ran ahead now, flanked by native dogs. The two Murani and I spread out fanwise, running behind.

Our first sign of warthog was the squeal of a baby surprised in a patch of grass by one of the mongrels. The squeal was followed by what seemed to be the squeals of all the baby warthogs in Africa, blended, magnified, and ear-splitting. Panic-stricken, the little pigs ran in all directions, like mice in the dream of a tabby cat. Their tails, held straight and erect, whisked through the grass as if so many bulrushes had come to life to join in a frantic dance—a mad and somewhat gay dance, but hardly as abandoned as it appeared, because the squeals were not without intent or meaning. They were meant for the small, alert ears of their father, who, when he came, would come with murder aforethought.

And come he did. None of us quite knew from where, but in the midst of the bedlam the grass in front of Arab Maina parted as if cleaved by a scythe, and a large boar, blind with rage, plunged from it straight at the Murani.

If Buller had not run ahead after his own quarry, things might have happened differently. As it was, there was more amusement than tragedy in what did happen.

The boar was larger than average, and the bigger they are the tougher they are. Their hides are tough as boot-leather and nothing less than a spear thrust in a vital part will stop them.

Arab Maina was ready and waiting. The boar lunged, the Murani side-stepped, the spear flashed—and the boar was gone. But not alone. Behind him, spitting the flying dust, swearing in Nandi and in Swahili, ran Arab Maina assisted by two of his mongrels—all of them following, with their eyes and their legs, the drunkenly swaying shaft of Arab Maina's spear, its point lodged fast and solid between the shoulders of the boar.

Arab Kosky and I began to follow, but we couldn't laugh and run at the same time, so we stopped running and watched. In less than a minute the dogs, the man, and the warthog had found the horizon and disappeared behind it like four fabulous characters in search of Æsop.

We turned and trotted in the direction Buller had taken, listening to his deep, excited barks which came at regular intervals. After covering about three miles, we found him at the side of a large hole where he had run his warthog to ground.

Buller stood gazing at the dusty opening in silence, as if hoping the warthog would be such a fool as to think that since there were no more barks, there was no more dog. But the warthog was not taken in. He would emerge in his own good time, and he knew as well as Buller did that no dog would enter an occupied pig-hole and expect to come out alive.

"That's a good boy, Buller!" As usual, I was relieved to find him still unhurt, but the moment I spoke, he broke his strategic silence and demanded, with much tail-wagging and a series of whining barks, that the warthog be roused from his den and be brought to battle.

More than once every inch of Buller's body had been ripped open in deep, ugly gashes on such pig-hunts, but at least he had lately learned not to go for the boar's head which, in the end, is fatal for any dog. Until now I had always managed to reach the scene of conflict in time to spear the warthog. But I might not always be so lucky.

I moved carefully to the back of the opening while Arab Kosky stood far to one side.

"If only we had some paper to rustle down the hole, Kosky . . ."

The Murani shrugged. "We will have to try other tricks, Lakweit."

It seems silly, and perhaps it is, but very often, after every other method had failed, we had enticed warthogs into the open, long before they were quite ready to attack, simply by rustling a scrap of paper over the entrance of their holes. It was not always easy to get so limited an article as paper in East Africa at that time, but when we had it, it always worked. I haven't any idea of why it worked. Poking a stick through the hole never did, nor shouting into it, nor even using smoke. To the warthog, I think, the paper made a sound that was clearly insulting—comparable perhaps to what is known here and there nowadays as a Bronx cheer.

But we had no paper. We tried everything else without the least success, and decided finally, in the face of Buller's contempt, to give it up and find out what had happened to Arab Maina on his quest for the vanished spear.

We were leaving the scene of our mutual discouragement when Arab Kosky's curiosity overcame his natural caution. He bent down in front of the dark hole and the warthog came out.

It was more like an explosion than an attack by a wild pig. I could see nothing through the thick burst of dust except extremities—the tail of the boar, the feet of Arab Kosky, the ears of Buller, and the end of a spear.

My own spear was useless in my hands. I might thrust at the warthog only to strike the dog or the Murani. It was an unholy tangle with no end, no beginning, and no opening. It lasted five seconds. Then the warthog shot from the tumbling mass like a clod from a whirlwind and disappeared through a corridor of anthills with Buller just behind slashing at the fleeing gray rump.

I turned to Arab Kosky. He sat on the ground in a puddle of his own blood, his right thigh cut through as if it had been hacked with a sword. He pressed a fold of his shuka against the wound and stood up. Buller's bark grew fainter, echoing through the forest of anthills. The boar had won the first battle—and might win the second, unless I hurried.

"Can you walk, Kosky? I must follow Buller. He may get killed."

The Murani smiled without mirth. "Of course, Lakweit! This is nothing—except reward for my foolishness. I will go back to the singiri slowly and have it attended to. It is best that you lose no time and follow Buller. Already the sun is sinking. Go now, and run quickly!"

I clasped the round shaft of the spear tight in my hand and ran with all my strength. For me—because I was still a child—this was a heart-sinking experience. So many thoughts flashed through my mind. Would my strength hold out long enough to save Buller from the tusks of the boar? What had become of Arab Maina, and why had I ever left him? How would poor Kosky get home? Would he bleed too badly on the way?

I ran on and on, following the barely audible bark of Buller, and the few drops of blood clinging at intervals to the stalks of grass or soaking into the absorbent earth. It was either Buller's blood or the warthog's. Most likely it was both.

"Ah-yey, if I could only run a little faster!"

I must not stop for a minute. My muscles begin to ache, my legs bleed from the "wait-a-bit" thorns and the blades of elephant grass. My hand, wet with perspiration, slips on the handle of my spear. I stumble, recover, and run on as the sound of Buller's bark grows louder, closer, then fades again.

The sun is going and shadows lay like broad hurdles across my path. Nothing is of any importance to me except my dog. The boar is not retreating; he is leading Buller away from me, away from my help.

The blood spoor grows thicker and there is more of it. Buller's bark is weak and irregular, but a little nearer. There are trees now jutting from the plain, large, solitary, and silent.

The barking stops and there is nothing but the blood to follow. How can there be so much blood? Breathless and running still, I peer ahead into the changing light and see something move in a patch of turf under a flat-topped thorn tree.

I stop and wait. It moves again and takes color—black and white and splattered with red. It is silent, but it moves. It is Buller.

I need neither breath nor muscles to cover the few hundred yards to the thorn tree. I am suddenly there, under its branches, standing in a welter of blood. The warthog, as large as any I have ever seen, six times as large as Buller, sits exhausted on his haunches while the dog rips at its belly.

The old boar sees me, another enemy, and charges once more with magnificent courage, and I sidestep and plunge my spear to his heart. He falls forward, scraping the earth with his great tusks, and lies still. I leave the spear in his body, turn to Buller, and feel tears starting to my eyes.

The dog is torn open like a slaughtered sheep. His right side is a valley of exposed flesh from the root of his tail to his head, and his ribs show almost white, like the fingers of a hand smeared with blood. He looks at the warthog, then at me beside him on my knees, and lets his head fall into my arms. He needs water, but there is no water anywhere, not within miles.

"Ah-yey! Buller, my poor, foolish Buller!"

He licks my hand, and I think he knows I can do nothing, but forgives me for it. I cannot leave him because the light is almost gone now and there are leopards that prowl at night, and hyenas that attack only the wounded and helpless.

"If only he lives through the night! If only he lives through the night!"

There is a hyena on a near hill who laughs at that, but it is a coward's laugh. I sit with Buller and the dead boar under the thorn tree and watch the dark come closer.

The world grows bigger as the light leaves it. There are no boundaries and no landmarks. The trees and the rocks and the anthills begin to disappear, one by one, whisked away under the magical cloak of evening, I stroke the dog's head and try to close my eyes, but of course I cannot. Something moves in the tall grass, making a sound like the swish of a woman's skirt. The dog stirs feebly and the hyena on the hill laughs again.

I let Buller's head rest on the turf, stand up, and pull my spear from the body of the boar. Somewhere to the left there is a sound, but I do not recognize it and I can see only dim shapes that are motionless.

I lean for a moment on my spear peering outward at what is nothing, and then turn toward my thorn tree.

"Are you here, Lakwani?"

Arab Maina's voice is cool as water on shaded rocks.

"I am here, Maina."

He is tall and naked and very dark beside me. His shuka is tied around his left forearm to allow his body freedom to run.

"You are alone, and you have suffered, my child."

"I am all right, Maina, but I fear for Buller. I think he may die."

Arab Maina kneels on the earth and runs his hands over Buller's body. "He is badly hurt, Lakwani—very badly hurt—but do not grieve too much. I think your spear has saved him from death, and God will reward you for that. When the moon shines at midnight, we will carry him home."

"I am so happy that you have come, Maina."

"How is it Kosky dared to leave you alone? He has betrayed the trust I had in him!"

"Do not be angry with Kosky. He is badly hurt. His thigh was ripped by the warthog."

"He is no child, Lakweit. He is a Murani, and he should have been more careful, knowing I was not there. After I recovered my spear, I turned back to find you. I followed the blood on the grass for miles—and then I followed Buller's barking. If the direction of the wind had been wrong, you would still be alone. Kosky has the brains of the one-eyed hare!"

"Ah-yey! What does it matter now, Maina? You are here, and I am not alone. But I am very cold."

"Lakwani, lie down and rest. I will keep watch until it is light enough for us to go. You are very tired. Your face has become thin."

He cuts handfuls of grass with his sword and makes a pillow, and I lie down, clasping Buller in my arms. The dog is unconscious now and bleeding badly. His blood trickles over my khaki shorts and my thighs.

The distant roar of a waking lion rolls against the stillness of the night, and we listen. It is the voice of Africa bringing memories that do not exist in our minds or in our hearts—perhaps not even in our blood. It is out of time, but it is there, and it spans a chasm whose other side we cannot see.

A ripple of lightning plays across the horizon.

"I think there will be a storm tonight, Maina."

Arab Maina reaches out in the darkness and puts his hand on my forehead. "Relax, Lakwani, and I will tell you an amusing fable about the cunning little Hare."

He begins very slowly and softly, "The Hare was a thief . . . In the night he came to the manyatta . . . He lied to the Cow, and told her that her Calf would die if she moved . . . Then he stood up on his hind legs and began sucking the milk from the Cow's milk bag . . . The other . . ."

But I am asleep.

# SHEEP HUNTING WITH OIL MAN JOHN

## Pam Houston

ABOUT A DECADE ago I was employed as a Dall sheep hunting guide in Alaska. I spent four seasons (August 10 to September 20) leading one or two men at a time into the Alaskan wilderness in pursuit of the wild sheep native to that part of North America. The men were primarily from Texas and Louisiana, and they had paid anywhere from ten to twenty thousand dollars each for a ten day solo hunt. My wage was a hundred dollars a day, and because our days began at three in the morning and rarely ended before midnight, I earned every penny.

Because my clients had spent the several months prior to the hunt behind a large desk earning multiples of the twenty thousand dollar trip fee, they weren't often in the kind of shape they would have liked to be for hiking up and over mountains and glaciers in Alaska. As a result, I often wound up carrying their gear as well as mine, and all of our food and equipment. I insisted each man carry his own gun, and most of them happily obliged.

I have written in other places about the several times when those ten day hunts turned into nightmares, overnights spent shivering on a glacier, or swollen and sweating in my sleeping bag after a bee sting's allergic reaction kicked in. I have written about the hunters for whom it was impossible to respect a woman guide, how in one case their disrespect cost them their shot at a trophy ram, and in another case left a dead ram at the bottom of a thousand foot glacial crevasse, its meat and horns irretrievable by all predators, human and otherwise. I have written about times when I felt a hunter was so undeserving, so clueless about the place he was and the animal he was chasing, that I threw the hunt in the sheep's favor. I was able to accomplish this without doing anything so dramatic as allowing the sheep to see or hear me, but only by holding my tongue when the hunter was about to stand and stretch, light a cigarette, or tell another off-color joke.

Sheep are smart. They are fast and agile rock climbers and their vision and sense of smell passes all human understanding. That's why sheep hunts are ten days, one hunter, one guide; nine out of every ten days and then some, the sheep are going to win. I have also written about the times the hunters win. About the pain of watching one of those miraculous snow white beings go down hard and fast with an accurate shot, when the silence that follows makes you want to swear there was never a life there to begin with. Or worse still, when they fall from a terrible shot and die slow and in agony, their bellies reeking already as the hole in their stomach poisons them from the inside.

The thing I've never written about is a hunt where everything went well. When I had trust, and genuine affection for the hunter I was guiding, when he had respect for me and the mountains where we camped. A time when I wanted the hunter to succeed even more than he did himself. When I got caught up in the spirit of the hunt, and unusually—even uncannily—attached to the outcome. When my desire for the hunter to kill an animal was stronger than my fear of watching it die.

There was such a time (though only one), and such a hunter. He was from Louisiana, and all he said about his profession was that he was "in oil." I guessed that didn't mean he actually worked out on the rigs.

It was September 1991, and he said that every day the Gulf War continued, his company earned another fifty grand. If I did remember his name, I'd probably make one up for him for the sake of his privacy. Because I don't remember it, I'll call him Oil Man John.

He was my last hunter of the season; that was my initial incentive. If I could get Oil Man John his sheep in a hurry, I was free to fly out of the mountains, get my first shower, my first salad, my first mattress, in more than six weeks. If we didn't get a sheep in the first seven days, I was going to fly out anyway, and my boss would take over with John for the final three days of the season. I intended to go visit my friend Lydia in Homer, eat some fresh halibut, visit the art galleries, remind myself that there was more to my life than crawling through streams on my belly and carefully carving the delicate skin and fur away from the eyeballs and cheekbones of a dead sheep.

John said if he got his ram early enough, he might be interested in seeing Homer, and maybe doing a little fishing. John was interested in everything: the way the tundra turned just a little more red and gold each morning, the blueberry patch were I got the berries for the sourdough pancakes we ate at three a.m., the ptarmigan— fat fluffy white and stupid birds that run underfoot saying "what the fuck, what the fuck," the occasional porcupine, wolf, moose, caribou, or grizzly bear that we'd pass in our daily pursuit of the sheep.

All week we hunted the upper drainage of the Little Delta River, one side canyon each day for six days. We saw a few rams, all of them too high to climb to, but John wasn't discouraged at all. He liked walking up each of the tundra and rock covered valleys just to see what they revealed: an abandoned stone cabin, a crystal spring, a thousand foot rock fall. He liked heading out early in the morning when what was left of the Alaskan summer's midnight sun was rolling back up over the lip of the horizon. He especially liked the long naps we'd take stretched out in our camouflage on the tundra during the warmest hours of the day when the sheep weren't moving at all.

It was on that seventh morning, the one that should have been my last in the mountains, when John told me he wanted to go to Homer with me, if I wouldn't mind. That if the truth be told, he wasn't all that gung ho of a hunter anyway, that he loved seeing the wolves and the moose and the mountains, that he had wanted to experience Alaska's rugged interior, and now he was ready for the coast.

You are probably suspicious, by now, that there was something flirtatious or romantic or even carnal going on between Oil Man John and me, but I have to tell you for the sake of the story that there was not. The type of man who would spend twenty thousand dollars to hunt sheep in Alaska is generally not turned on by the type of woman who would be paid $100.00 a day to guide that hunt. In fact, most of my clients were a little scared to sleep in the same tent with me, as if I was, say, an alien being of some kind. John was neither frightened of me nor interested. He seemed to have the same kind of respect for my outdoorsmanship that I had for the spirit with which he came to the outdoors.

We woke up from our nap on that seventh afternoon. The sun was hot on a big soft patch of still green tundra we'd found, and we had slept long and hard after a four a.m. start. John was tired and shower deprived and ready to call it a day, call it a hunt, ready to go halibut fishing.

"Come on," I said, "let's just see what's around this next corner." My strategy when hunters got lazy was to help them up the hill with a mental short rope. I'd get a hundred yards above them, let them catch up eighty or ninety, say a few encouraging words and then stretch the distance to a hundred yards again.

"Pam," John said, "It's okay about the sheep. Right now all my fantasies involve massages and big red bottles of wine."

"Let's just go up till we can see behind that next big boulder." I said, "I have a feeling about it."

The weird thing was, I *did* have a feeling about it, but those were the kinds of feelings I always kept to myself.

"If we don't see anything from there," I said, "then we'll call it a hunt."

This is the part where I get a little squeamish. All season long I'd been marching around the tundra with hunters who got so nervous if their gun didn't go off in the first three days that they started taking pot shots at the ptarmigan (which are so easy to kill a child could do it with a well aimed rock). The hunters had gotten their sheep or they hadn't, because of me or in spite of me. One thing I'd never imagined myself doing was dragging a hunter up the steepest part of a valley when he would have been just as happy to go home with a three-hundred-and-fifty-pound fish.

We reached the boulder and behind it and across the valley we saw two grazing rams. They saw us too and started to climb immediately, but the valley was narrow enough to shoot across, so we started to climb up our side.

The first thing that needed to happen before John took a shot was that I had to determine, with binoculars or a spotting scope, whether either of the animals we encountered met the legal definition of a "harvestable" ram. For a ram to be legal in our game district, it had to be either eight years old, or wearing horns that made a full curl, or wearing horns that were broken back on both sides, indicating years of growth and fighting. Unlike deer, moose, and caribou, which drop their antlers each year, wild sheep spend their whole lives growing one set of horns. The new growth pushes the old growth out some inches each year until the horns get so long they curl. You can count a sheep's age by the growth rings on his horns, but that's a lot easier up close after the ram is no longer moving. The full curl judgment is tricky from a distance as well, because what looks like a full curl from above or below can change when you are viewing it, as the regulation book tells you to, straight on, through the eye. The hunter's guidelines change the wording almost every year trying to come up with a definition that everyone can agree upon, and the game wardens fly all over the area making sure nobody bends the rules.

The game warden in our unit—a man with a name like Bunselmeyer—made himself famous a few years prior by going sheep hunting with his wife. She spotted a ram, got out her spotting scope out and asked for his opinion about whether or not it was a legal ram.

"You're the hunter," he said, "you make the call."

She shot the ram, and when they went to retrieve it the warden felt it wasn't quite making the book definition of a full curl.

He arrested his wife on the spot, the story goes, sent her to jail and fined her fifteen thousand dollars.

Both of the rams Oil Man John and I saw that day looked like full curls through my binoculars. Neither of them looked like they were making it by much. The one in the lead had more mass in his horns, while the second ram's curl was small and tight. It was a long shot across the valley. John was shooting a Remington .270, and only felt comfortable in the 200–250 yard range. We agreed in whispers that it was a 250-yard shot, both knowing in our hearts it was more like three hundred. A clearer shot could not have been imagined; there was nothing between us and the ram except high thin air.

"If you think you've got the shot," I said, "go ahead and take it."

I thought of all the hunters I'd seen choke over four seasons of guiding. The world champion skeet shooter who missed entirely from thirty yards and then gut shot the ram spoiling nearly all of the meat. The Texan who bragged to me that he had shot six elk in five minutes from the driver's seat of his truck, who made such a poor shot that my boss had to track the sheep for three days before it finally died.

Oil Man John had said he wasn't all that much of a hunter, but something told me he wouldn't take a shot he didn't feel pretty good about.

I heard the crack of the .270 and the ram fell dead without so much as a breath. This was the moment when all the other hunters whooped so loud that every living creature within a hundred square miles headed over to the next valley. I waited, but John was silent.

"Great shot," I said, but John just stared at the dead ram.

"That was a long 250 yards," he said. He looked, for just a second, like he wished he hadn't pulled the trigger.

"You nailed it," I said, shaking his hand. "You should be very proud of that shot."

"Yes," he said, the corner of his mouth turning in to a smile, "I guess I really am."

"Let's go get your ram," I said, "It's looking like a storm."

And it was. What had been wispy mare's tails of clouds all afternoon had grown gray edges and sharp lines. You could see the north wind in the curl of the dark cloud at the edge of the front.

Going to get the ram proved more difficult than we imagined. The canyon wall where the sheep had fallen was considerably steeper than the one we had climbed, something I should have taken into account before I let John fire. It took an hour of crawling, digging our fingers and boot toes into the near vertical tundra, grabbing on to the skinny twigs that more often than not pulled out into our hands. By the time we reached the ram we were breathless, clinging to the steep side of the canyon, and fat white flakes were falling from the sky.

"We're never going to be able to gut it properly at this angle," I said, "Let's roll it down to the valley floor and cut it up there."

The next fifteen minutes were vintage Laurel and Hardy, or maybe the Three Stooges, if you count one stooge as the sheep. On its way to the canyon floor the ram either picked up not enough momentum or way too much. At first it caught itself on every branch and hummock, places that were nearly impossible to get to, to set it free. Then it started falling so fast that I was afraid we'd damage the horns or cape so I threw my body in front of it and got its legs wrapped around me somehow, and we tumbled together all blood and mud and death ooze all the way to the valley floor.

By the time John got his camera put away and stopped laughing, there were four new inches of snow on the ground. By the time we had the sheep cleaned and gutted, we were standing in more than a foot. I've lived at high elevation all my adult life, but I had never seen snow pile up as fast as it did that afternoon.

"You know, the sheep isn't that important," John said, "Let's leave it here and mark the spot somehow and get back to the tent while we can still walk. It's not worth dying over. We can always come back up here tomorrow."

We both knew that depended on the weather, and if it snowed all night at this magnitude, there wouldn't be anybody going up that valley till spring.

There's a law in Alaska called the Wanton Waste Law that states that it is illegal to transport an animal's horns without also carrying the meat. If all a hunter wants is a trophy, he's got to prove he carried the majority of the meat from the animal out of the bush and gave it to a Fish and Game approved charity. That same game warden who arrested his wife has been known to get on airplanes with people all the way back to Texas just to see if their checked luggage has plenty of frozen meat to go with those carried-on horns. Luckily, John wanted to take sheep steaks home as much as he wanted the horns and cape, so grabbing the head and making a run for it never came up for discussion.

The snow was raising more serious questions in our minds, like how, if eight or nine feet piled up over night, we'd get from the tent the ten miles down to the tiny river rock airstrip. And how, if they got anything close to that amount down valley, our pilot would be able to land.

That morning we'd been sleeping in the sun dreaming of lattes in Homer; now we were contemplating being snow bound for ten months with nothing to eat but a sheep and a few left over boxes of Jell-O pudding. We dressed the nearest tree in orange like it was Christmas and high tailed it through one and then two and then three feet of snow back to the tent. I felt terrible about leaving the ram, but I also knew fall storms were often fierce and abbreviated, and there was a good chance the snow would stop and we would be able to go back for it. If not, John said, he'd made an early donation to the wolves' spring feedathon.

The tent was a welcome sight but as we shivered in it all night, Homer seemed like a dream forgotten. I woke up to a 3 a.m. that was so cold I knew the sky had to have cleared. We woke a second time to a blue and white universe, all the reds and oranges and goldenrod buried under drifts of snow. But the creek sparkled through all silver and sapphire, and by the time we finished breakfast the sun had warmed the snow enough for it to settle. It took only another six hours to go back up the valley and reclaim our ram, which had been buried entirely, except for one black skyward turned hoof.

The entire time I've been writing this essay, I've been hoping some concluding thoughts would have made themselves known to me by now. That I would be able to explain why, in four seasons of guiding, every animal's death that I had a hand in made me grief-stricken and nauseated and entirely full of self loathing—save one.

I would like to be able to write a convincing paragraph proving that because of Oil Man John's symbiotic relationship with nature, his ram's death was the completion of a sacred cycle, that the ram was subsumed inside him, remade as part of his life experience, and therefore not lost at all. I could hypothesize that it was his *not* wanting the ram that allowed him to have it without psychic consequences, that his brief mourning of the ram at the death (unique in my experience of hunters) was further proof of his worthiness. I could employ all manner of New Age thought to convince you that it was perfectly all right for Oil Man John's ram to die, and perfectly all right for me to lead him to it. But in the end it all winds up sounding like the rationalizations of dictators and despots. Hitler logic. Khomeini speak.

I realize there is no way to talk about any of this without feeling deeply ashamed. Of the four hunters I guided that season, three went home with rams, and one did not, and I am ashamed of the fact that I grieved the first two rams deeply, and John's ram almost not at all. Of the three hunters that killed, only John, in my opinion, was worthy of his trophy (the other two hunters, of course, would feel differently), and I am ashamed of myself for presuming to know who should be allowed to kill and who shouldn't. The hunter who did not kill had no business at all being in the woods, and I am ashamed that I took such good care of him that he lived to inflict himself upon some other guide and some other group of animals.

At my home in the San Juan Mountains we've had a moose visit us several times in the last few weeks. He's big, nearly as big as an Alaskan Moose, and he'll pop up unexpectedly next to the horse trough when I go out to fill it in the evening, or right next to the homesteader's cabin, hunkering like bad news in the early morning fog. We're smack dab in the middle of moose season here in Colorado, which is only nine days long, and by drawing only. By the end of the week I'll have spent more time praying that our moose avoids the fate of Oil Man John's ram, than I will have doing anything else.

It has been more than ten years since I guided my last hunter, since I stopped doing something for a living that I am even more conflicted about than prostituting my life to the written word. I wish I could say that time has clarified my reasons for guiding, that the intervening years have reconciled my pride in my skills and endurance at that time and the vast amount of wilderness knowledge I gained in Alaska with my bewilderment about my own participation in a sport as ghastly as trophy hunting. But they have not. I'd like to believe I would never try to dictate who deserves to kill, and what deserves to die, but that is precisely what I have done in this essay. The only thing that seems consistent in me is my addiction to contradiction. I am probably the only registered hunting guide in the history of Alaska that has never actually shot at anything alive.

My enduring hope is that all my unresolvable conflicts are gifts from the universe, opportunities to become more tolerant, more honest, more fair.

Even that I can't be sure of. Because if some yahoo from Oklahoma shoots our moose this week and I hear the gunfire, I'm going to have a hard time not shooting back.

# HEART OF THE HUNT

## Allen Morris Jones

HUNTING REQUIRES OPTIMISM. You get up at five o'clock, walk until eleven, rest, and hunt again until dark only because the next hunt is the *one*.

I walk from the house on a path I have already traveled four or five times this season. I'll be walking around beneath the grain fields through the Breaks in order to come up onto the flat fields from the unexpected below.

These early snows always make it look like it should be a lot colder than it is. A light skiff erases surfaces without being enough to cover the edges, and the horizontal arrangement gives the world a tough cast.

I bugle below the first field, staring up at the scalloped horizon, and am met with silence. After a few minutes, I move farther along, just below the next set of fields, and bugle again. Immediately there's a deep, mature response, and then two higher ones, from satellite bulls. They're not close, but they're there.

Genetic or associational, can there be any greater feeling of anticipation than in the first moments of a stalk? Your eyes bulge with sudden adrenaline and you find yourself taking note of the slightest currents of wind, the smallest movements of brush, the most incidental flights of birds. All this even while your conscious attention is focused on the animal in front of you. You are *awake.*

A smaller bull bugles again, perhaps a little farther away. I pick up speed.

The snow has started to melt, and by the time I reach the base of the hill below the field, I'm walking on layered stilts of gumbo and snow. I stand to scrape the clods off and look up to see a small five-point bull craning its head down at me.

I freeze, holding my breath to small pulses.

Five minutes and the bull grows impatient, turning finally back to the herd, out of sight.

Nothing to do but play it through.

In the timber I bugle again, to keep the bull from spooking and to fix the positions of the other elk. Somehow, there is an answer. And then several answers—all above me and still in the field.

Hunting alone, the nature of possible scenarios changes dramatically. Last year with my father, a bull hung up seventy or eighty yards out and began circling us for our scent. I backed up, breaking limbs and grunting. Dad stayed ahead, behind a juniper bush. The bull was encouraged enough by my retreat to come on in, spooking only as Dad rattled his arrow across a branch. But alone, with no bugler to distract the bull, quiet stalking is often the best.

If you are hunting well, the state of inclusion comes to perpetuate itself. To fulfill your project, you need to know the land, what forms it takes and how you can work with them. To kill your bull, you need to know the animal, his habits and abilities to avoid you. Most important, you need to know yourself, how far you can reason-

166

ably walk in a day, how quietly you can stalk. Some hunters announce themselves with trumpets while a very few can slip through the woods in their suits of rustling leaves and trickling water.

If I could move around in front, below them, I might be able to lay an ambush from a narrow finger of timber that I know is there, connecting the field to the ravine.

I scrabble along the sidehill for half a mile before topping out into a string of timber.

The herd is already spread out in the open, not as close to the timber as I had hoped and still over a hundred yards away. A few of the cows are looking in my direction, ears alert. A few more are in the timber. I freeze. At the end of the line, a good six-point, larger than the earlier bull, stretches his nose out to a cow.

There's no way I can make it around to another ambush without attracting attention. I try a cow call. Twenty heads and a pair of antlers swivel toward me. The cows stand still and the bull steps back and forth, wanting to run, wanting to give chase, but unwilling to leave his cows.

There is a movement off to my left. Two elk that I hadn't seen, a raghorn and the five point, stand at the edge of the timber on my side, less than seventy yards away. I ease to the side and put a small tree between me and the two bulls, hoping the herd won't spook at my movement.

Cow call again. I lift my bow and prepare to draw, broadhead trembling. Their steps are heavy through the wet grass and I can smell their musky odor. The raghorn steps out fifteen yards away, staring directly at me. His nostrils quiver. I wait. I can't breathe. I can hear the five point walking up close behind him. He steps between me and the raghorn. Ten yards away, no more. After a few seconds, a few hours, they both turn to look at the herd on the other side of the field. I draw and shoot.

And I die a little as the arrow goes in high. Sometimes the very short distances can be harder than the very long.

But the despair turns into elation as I watch the elk stumble as he runs into the timber. The brush crashes.

The elation turns to sadness: success, but failure.

I sit down. My trembling hands move like flags over my face, over the ground, into my pockets.

A badly wounded elk, if it doesn't die immediately, will usually go only a short distance before lying down, sick. If given enough time, maybe just a few minutes, it will die there. If it's forced to keep walking, it can walk its wounds away. I expect to find this one lying just inside the trees. But I've been wrong before.

I'm confident that crash came when he fell. Almost confident. I stand and walk through the field to the timber on the other side.

Twenty feet within the timber, where the steep banks cut into the sun, and the temperature drops until I can see my breath, I find the arrow lying unbroken on an open patch of needles. Thirty feet farther on I see an antler curving up out of a deadfall.

I wish there was someone with me, someone else looking, so I could holler back that I've found him and that he's a good one— just to holler. I do it anyway; it feels wrong not to.

Caught in the brush, the antlers twist his head back as if he were just now getting ready to bugle.

I find a place on the dead log slightly above him and sit down, grabbing the antler between the third and fourth points. Solid. Cool.

His legs stretch out in mid-stride, black enough to carry a reflection. That's what has been making the tracks I've seen. The thick, knotted hair across his stomach stinks of mud and urine.

Hunting is not an attempt to take possession of the animal, as so many hunters have argued. If that were the case, the attempt is doomed to absolute failure.

I cannot possess the elk. It's dead. But I can possess the memory of it in the moment before I killed it, which is enough. It's more than enough. What I have brought away is my relationship to the animal, not the animal itself.

It is not so much a desire to possess as to *be* possessed.

And to be possessed, you must hunt him. To hunt him, you must kill him. The words of this hard verity are etched arrow-deep into every sandstone bluff, screamed by every dying rabbit, whispered against the cheek of every hunter. We fight for the right to live, marking out our territory in a spray of blood, reddening our teeth and nails on life-truths.

And in front of me now, arrested, lies a dead mass of energy. But it is dead only until it flows back into the process, through me.

Its stomach faces the downhill side. Good luck.

I take off my pack and jacket, roll up my sleeves, break off a few branches to clear the way, and open my knife. Alone, with no one to pull back on the ribcage or arrange its legs, this is going to be a dirtier job than usual.

Beginning in the middle of the stomach, slightly off to one side to avoid the thickest of the hair, I make a small incision with the edge of the blade. A few inches away and the white paunch presses out. I slide my first two fingers down into the incision, placing the knife between them, edge up, and make a single long cut up to its ribcage. The paunch expands, pulled by gravity, and when I go back and cut down the pelvic area, it spills out: stomach, upper intestine, the first lobes of the liver, the small knot of the gallbladder. The rest is obscured by a warm wash of blood that swallows my hands and lower arms.

The arrow went in high, it died almost immediately, there's all this blood . . . I must have sliced the aorta.

The pancreas, the thick neck of the lower intestine, the hard kidneys; these come out next. I reach blindly back up and cut almost randomly, severing all the connections that I can feel. Two of the four or five scars on my fingers have come from this kind of cutting. The largest portion of viscera, now free, slides out into the dead branches.

The year has been wet enough and the growing season long enough that his fat lays in chunks everywhere; my hands are greasy.

I reach back and carefully extract the bowel and then the bladder, clamping it shut with my thumb and forefinger. Only then do I move back to the testicles, which can give the meat an unpleasant flavor if left close.

For the sternum, I take out and assemble the small game-saw I've been carrying all these weeks. It will let me empty the chest cavity of lungs, heart, and esophagus without getting bloody past the elbows: an indulgent nicety.

Another wash of aortal blood.

Blood is six times heavier than water. A bull like this carries five to six gallons of it. If I were Cree I would drink a few swallows to keep from being disturbed by the sight of it in battle.

Within the chest, the lungs are flaccid and spongy, holding their strong lines of contour even as I cut them apart. Inflated, they have the capacity of six gallons.

The blood has spread from the carcass in an expanding arc and soaked through one of my pant legs, turning it tacky and stiff.

I remove the ten-pound heart, still twitching with its physical memory. If I were Crow, I would set it aside as a gesture of respect. I do it anyway.

It's a distancing mechanism, this knowledge. But you have to go through it, just like you have to read the billboards driving through town. The necessity of killing does not make you any happier doing it, not after you are conscious of yourself.

To remove the cape, I make a cut from the sternum to the top of the shoulder, then another from the crest of the back to a point between and slightly behind the antlers. This done, I grab the corner at the shoulder and pull it away, cutting. Fat stands in layers above the skull.

With the cape hanging loose, I cut and twist the neck vertebrae just below the skull, removing the head and setting it aside. Its eyes fall back into its skull. If I were a Flathead, I would close them.

I cut away the front shoulders and rear hips at the joints, laying them on a plastic bag to be boned later. The straps, loins, and ribs I will have to do here.

For the back straps, I remove the skin and make two cuts along the top ridge of the vertebrae (the knife bouncing along the contours of the bone) and horizontally above the ribs. A cut at the front and back and the strap is cleanly off. Next, I saw the largest series of ribs away from the vertebrae and then use this new space to get to the internal loins.

The elk, now little more than a backbone and a half of a ribcage, is easy to turn over for the other strap and ribs.

I lay the four legs and ribs to one side, covering them with an orange plastic tarp. I tie the head, straps, and loins onto my pack frame. It's heavy, but the cabin's no more than three or four miles away. Once home, I'll be able to drive the truck back to within a hundred yards to pick up the legs and ribs. Truthfully, I wouldn't have to pack out anything. But it's a way of paying dues.

Almost exactly two hours after hearing the first bugle, I begin hiking back to the cabin.

*Part Eight*

# ONE DAY NEAR MARILAL
## (for Lambat)

### Dan Gerber


We needed meat for the camp, and
never having killed anything big, I wanted
to know what it meant to skin and clean a life,
and to eat it to stay alive.

But this death would have been too easy,
this beautiful impala, this dúme*,
who presented himself in the first half hour
as though it had all been arranged.

I eased the rifle down.

This wasn't what I thought it would be,
I told Bill. I would only do this once,
and there had to be more to it than this.

But in our tracker's black face, a black rage was growing.
You go back to America, he said.
You take pictures.

This dúme would have been dinner for us all.
He doesn't want to kill something like an impala.
Something beautiful. Bill tried to explain.
He wants to kill something ugly,
like a wart hog.

The tracker drew himself up like a cobra
and looked off toward the afternoon hills.

Beautiful, he said, as if a word to learn.
Beautiful or ugly, the heart is one.

---

*Dúme* (do-may): the Swahili word for the male of the herd.

# KILLING THE NEURAL PATHWAYS

John Jerome

LAST SUMMER A hawk savaged a nest in our backyard maple, taking at least one adult cedar waxwing, and in the process dumping four unfledged chicks onto the lawn. We couldn't see any sign of a surviving parent. I climbed the maple, hoping to put the chicks back, but couldn't find the nest. We couldn't figure out a way to feed them. My wife said I'd have to take care of the matter—she couldn't do it—and went into the house. "Put them down," as we say with pets, may have been the phrase she used.

A hammer blow, instantaneous, would have been the most merciful, but I didn't have the stomach for it, and chose to drown them instead, a grievous error. The struggle of each fluffy handful went on much longer than I expected. As the flutter moved from my hand up my arm to my brain, it put me musing on which synapses, which neural pathways, were being reinforced.

They were not new pathways; they were already in place. I grew up in the rural South, killing things with little compunction. I've

*177*

hunted, fished, participated in what is euphemistically called pest control. God knows how many animals I've run over in a lifetime of driving. I always swat biting insects, with a fierce, revengeful pleasure when I succeed.

I eat meat; I've done my share of butchering. My mother and her three Oklahoma sisters had four distinct methods for killing chickens, and I learned and practiced them all. (The most humane was hanging the bird by its feet and slitting its throat, which was also the least messy. The most bizarre was putting a broomstick across the bird's neck as it lay on the ground, standing on the broomstick, and pulling on its feet.)

I've put down dogs—and in that act, if not before, compunction begins to arise. Even when it was an act of mercy, or what I judged to be mercy, the judgment began to call itself into question. I've killed animals, or had them killed, to solve problems—beaver and other rodents, incontinent and crippled pets. Problem-solving by killing, however, is where the slope starts getting slippery. It begins leaking over into the category of murder.

One of my best friends is a lifelong hunter and fisherman. He is also a surgeon, and therefore surely knows a great deal more about death, as well as life, than I ever will. I don't challenge him on his avocations. I think I can understand, if not empathize with, the alleged bond between hunter and prey, the religio-mystical union. I admire the Native American tradition of asking the animal's forgiveness (or the tree's, for that matter, before you chop it down). I have no quarrel with that. I don't like loutish hunters, but then I don't like loutish vegetarians either. It's not the people, it's the act.

To quote Muhammad Ali on the matter of the Viet Cong, I am nonviolent toward fish, having no quarrel with them. That's what I used to say when the subject of fishing came up, but it was an evasion. Being a lifelong swimmer, I have a bond of my own with the species. It is not in the least mystical. Swimming with fish is a particular pleasure, as close a contact with other species as I am privileged to experience outside our household companion animals. I get no greater pleasure from the natural world than swimming along a coral reef, aswirl in its colorful inhabitants. I *love* fish.

I've caught them, but not in a long time. I don't like to. Back in the 1950s I used to know sportsmen who spoke of "killing" trout rather than just catching them, although I presume that quaint turn of phrase is no longer politically correct. It puzzled me at the time, but I suppose it was more honest, "catching" being after all a euphemism. Or at least it used to be, before the catch-and-release ethic caught hold. But I understand killing trout (they are delicious) better than I do catching them and then letting them go. I've heard the dubious argument that fish don't feel the hook, which is hard to imagine, given that a fish's entire physical body—skin, scales, fins, mouth, eyes, barbels, gills, *everything*—is in effect a quivering sensory organ.

In a novel I read back in the Fifties—unfortunately I remember neither title nor author—an adolescent boy, practicing casting on dry land, unthinkably flips his plug in front of his dog, and the dog snatches it up. The hook sinks in, the dog yelps, and bolts. The boy can't reel in the dog, can't stand doing that, so he is reduced to running after it, trying to keep the line slack, trying to catch the dog to remove the hook. The panicked dog won't let him. They run each other to exhaustion. Finally the boy lets the rod go, and the dog runs away, dragging rod and line behind him.

I don't remember the resolution of the incident, but I remember the tale every time I hear about the supposedly unfeeling mouth of a fish. I've had a fish on the line; I've felt that struggle. Fishermen, as I understand it, enjoy that feeling. They refer to it as "fight," and choose their target prey by which species struggle hardest. It's the real reason I don't like catching fish: I'm squeamish, I suppose. I can put a worm on the hook just fine (there's a dubious kind of specism at work here, something to do with skeletal muscles—and neural pathways, or my own vague notion of neural pathways). I just don't like the feeling of a live thing hurting itself in trying to escape my clutches. It forces me to consider what right I have to be clutching. This makes me uncomfortable.

What I really can't understand about catch-and-release is catching a fish—putting it through that trauma—just for the catching, for the infliction of that trauma. Then letting it go. What could be the sport in torturing fish?

When it comes to hunting, I'm willing to buy the argument that the "harvesting" of game animals by sportsmen can be more humane than death by fang and claw—although my sympathies are more with natural processes, which have been going on a lot longer than we've had high-velocity ammunition and telescopic sights. The prey species have to be better adapted by now to those more natural processes. But I'd rather see deer dispatched and eaten by respectful sportsmen than suffer a slow death by starvation. In either case the deer reenters the food chain. At our level there just happens to be a lot less need, and more waste. Wouldn't it be nice if each fall's so-called deer harvest could go directly to starving Third World populations—if it's not going to go directly back into the forest?

My problem with killing animals for sport rather than meat is a larger but perhaps more nebulous issue. It has to do with those neural pathways: with what transpires in the organism that is myself at the moment when the neural pathways shut down in the organism that is put to death. The hunting culture—the equipment, the tracking, the training of dogs, the detailed understanding of wildlife and the natural world—the tradition, the whole ball of wax—seems worthy, even honorable to me. It is how carnivorous mankind has fed itself from prehistoric time. But it ends in a transaction that needs to be deeply understood.

To be the agent of that transaction—that moment—carries more responsibility than I think we are willing to take on. It is a moment that, if consciously witnessed, consciously accepted, changes us. Maybe those who kill for sport do experience that change, and acknowledge it each time it happens. ("Experience" here is a less emotional word for "feel.") Maybe there are no casual killers among sportsmen. Having been one myself, I am forced to think otherwise.

Whatever the case, it seems to me that it should be possible for all of us to interrupt those particular neural pathways. They serve no purpose, at least for those of us not in the killing professions. There are other recreations. Perhaps none offer the emotional charge of killing, but that might be a level of emotional charge we could better live without. Neural pathways are maintained by repetition. My own has been interrupted long enough that it is now a shock to try to force its reconnection. I've lived with that neural pathway intact, and I've lived with it interrupted, and I find my life better—I am happier, easier, more comfortable in my skin—in the latter state. To reconnect it is increasingly painful, increasingly distressful. I find this instructive.

I don't hold this as a moral position. I'll leave the sanctity-of-life arguments to others. I just think that killing forms, or at least reinforces, the wrong neural pathways. My use of the term "neural pathways" is of course pseudo-scientific. I am referring to what other even less scientific but perhaps deeper thinkers—certainly more moralistically inclined thinkers—refer to as the Soul.

That is, I'm not so worried about what it does to the animals; I'm worried about what it does to us. My wife and I live in a very nice patch of New England woods. It supports black bear, deer, porcupine, coyote, fox skunk, fisher, raccoon, rabbit, wild turkey. The usual suspects. We delight in sharing it with anyone who wants to come onto land. It is posted only against motor vehicles, which disturb the habitat, and recreational killing, which disturbs the soul.

# THE HUNTER'S DANCE

## Louis Owens

I WAS HALFWAY across the Black River on a perfect, early summer day, thigh deep in the easy current and letting my vision drift thought-lessly up the grass of the opposite bank. Ponderosa pines laid dark, wavering lines on the canyon slope, and in the bright noon sunlight between two oblong shadows my eyes stopped on a doe and a coy-ote fighting for the life of a newborn fawn. With the breeze in my direction, and the utter focus of this life-battle, neither deer nor coyote noticed me a couple hundred feet away in the water.

Upright on precarious hind legs, the whitetail doe sparred with the coyote, jabbing spindly forelegs at his retreating face. Behind the deer, a miniscule spotted fawn lay tightly against a big log, push-ing itself as far into the crease between log and earth as it could get, doing precisely what its mother had ordered. The coyote feinted and dodged and retreated as the doe advanced in her awkward, fencing stance. And then, when he had lured her sufficiently far from the fawn, he suddenly raced around her and slashed at the baby, ripping a gash along the tiny neck and shoulder before the mother could wheel and drive him away. Again he teased the doe until she was too far from her newborn, whereupon he dove and slashed and retreated.

I knew I should do nothing, told myself sternly to just turn away. A voyeur, I should not even be watching this casual death, should not transform the uncomplicated reality of this thing into a dreadful aesthetic. This was a reality beyond anything I could judge or affect. For more time than I could comprehend, coyotes had taken new fawns from their mothers. The winter and spring had been particularly wet, and forage was rich and thick. Nature had responded to plenty with plenty, and rabbits were everywhere, coveys of quail exploding from every chokecherry and wild grape thicket, wild turkeys flocking with crowds of scurrying chicks. All over the White Mountain Apache reservation on this trip I'd seen does with late-born fawns, sometimes twins. The abundant coyotes, like the large dark male on the hillside above, were fat and sleek. The vignette I was witnessing had taken place uncountable times and would, God willing, take place uncountable more times long after I was compost.

Maybe it was my anthropocentric conviction that the coyote was grinning, enjoying the game it surely could not lose as it teased the doe away from the fawn. Maybe it was the fact of the mother's desperate courage in facing the formidable coyote, that complication by a mother's instinct of the clean line between predator and prey. Or perhaps it was just an inexcusable human weakness, blindness, or selfishness that converted everything into personal significance. For whatever reason, I banged my aluminum fly rod case loudly against a rock in the middle of the stream, leaving a sharp dent in the case and a crass metallic noise echoing in the otherwise silent canyon.

Coyote and deer paused and turned toward me and then in an instant both were gone, vanished over opposite sides of the low ridge. As quickly as I could with a heavy backpack, I waded out of the river and climbed up to the log. Slashed deeply in several places, the fawn, perhaps hours old, was in shock and doomed there in the hot sun. Already, flies buzzed around the hardening blood that covered its spotted sides. Already the eyes were glazed.

I walked away, feeling utterly stupid and impotent. The doe, I knew, would never return, traumatized as she was not only by her battle but perhaps even more so by my sudden, awful presence. The coyote, who like all coyotes considered man merely a temporary inconvenience, would return and enjoy the meal he'd earned. I would hike out to my truck and drive to Alpine, a little elk-hunting town two hours away, for the burger I always bought in the same café on my way back to Albuquerque after each trip down to the river. The doe, with such fawn loss undoubtedly programmed into her genetic code, would very likely bear again and try again to preserve the small life give to her. More fawns would fall prey to the same coyote who looked to be in his prime.

The day before, my fourth day on the small river, I had fished upstream from my camp, walking, wading, and casting, all thought and energy focused on reading water and catching fish, so that when I finally noticed the sun declining above the deep canyon I was three or four miles from my tent. I turned and began to retrace my steps, casting indifferently here and there just to see my brown and gray fly touch perfect pools and eddies. I'd already kept two rainbow trout for dinner and released many others, and I had no great interest in catching more fish.

I'd walked maybe a quarter of a mile when I saw the first lion tracks. Nearly as large as my outstretched hand, they were superimposed over the boot tracks I'd left as I meandered upstream, their softly rounded and surprisingly deep imprints looking precise and quite deliberate. As I tracked myself back toward camp, it became clear that the cougar had tracked me for over two miles, stepping where I'd stepped. Since I'd moved very slowly for those miles, stopping and casting and catching and releasing trout, studying currents and shadowy riffles, the cat must have moved even more slowly, must have stalked and toyed with me from a discrete distance, pausing where I paused, watching me with the same intensity I had watched the dark water, perhaps cocking an ear toward the splashing fish I magically drew from the stream. All cats are curious, including mountain lions, and the cougar might have just found me an interesting anomaly, an entertaining spectacle worth wasting a couple of hours on. It might have been a fairly young cat who had not seen a man before and was intrigued. But most likely, given the realpolitik of nature, the cougar was contemplating me as dinner. Abundant evidence has taught us that the great cats have very little difficulty placing humans within their spectrum of viable meals. Mountain lions, a naturalist friend had told me, have evolved canine teeth designed to fit precisely into the interstitial spaces between the vertebrae of deer just over the medulla oblongata, bringing a quick and efficient death. Would the same fit work the same inevitable magic upon my neck, I wondered? I felt strangely flattered to imagine myself thus accepted into a cougar's world, to be granted such a place of respect along with the deer and elk. But then, had the lion elected to sample my flavor I undoubtedly would have felt less flattered, and perhaps, I had to admit, I was still walking toward my camp precisely because I was not sufficiently part of that world. Maybe I had been spared because unlike those other creatures I had lost my rightful place. Or, finally, maybe it was nothing more complicated or subtle than the nine-foot graphite fly rod that saved me, a strange, waving antenna the cat was not disposed to mess with.

Two hours after I left the dying fawn, I was driving back toward New Mexico, up the spine of the White Mountains, pondering what had taken place. What kind of god, I wondered, would decree that coyotes should live by the horrific demise of a creature just hours old, by the pain of a mother incapable of protecting her young? What kind of moral universe decreed that countless millions of animals must experience terror and death in the beaks and jaws of other animals, every day, every hour, everywhere, until the natural state of the earth, it seemed, must be a single unending shriek of pain? The same god that caused the cougar, that magnificent creature of sinewy tendons and killing instincts, to contemplate me as sustenance, potential energy to drive those killing muscles? There's nothing like a sudden awakening to the fact that you are part of the food chain to cast a new light on things. And not a few human beings have had the privilege of actually being eaten by mountain lions.

In long retrospect, I ask other questions. What kind of god would decree that on my way back from the river I should stop in Alpine for a hamburger made of the ground flesh of a cow raised for that purpose, hormone-fed and fattened in muddy feedlots, crowded into stockyards with eyes gouged out by jostling horns, and finally lined into slaughterhouse factories to be killed with the sounds and smells of myriad other deaths in its ears and nostrils? For five days I had camped on the river, catching trout every day and releasing most, but every day selecting two or three fish to kill and cook for dinner. What god gave those trout lives into my hands? What kind of angry god has put so many lives at the disposal of others, the multitudinous rabbits mere grain for the predators? Is there a code to govern such infinite and necessary deaths, values by which we live and make die?

It is in the end the awful beauty of the dance of deer and coyote that I remember best from that summer day. The magnificent, futile courage of the doe, precarious on hind feet and jabbing hooves, and the luring, masterful control of the coyote. A *pas de deux* of death on one hand and a mere coyote lunch on the other. A pain so great it seems even today to rend the air I breathe, but whose pain? A fearful, perfect symmetry. My own minuet with mountain lion strikes me as a passing grace, a brief moment of near acceptance, a question unanswered.

I grew up hunting. We were a poor family of nine children, and the little income our father could make as a ranch hand or truck driver did not go far. The year I entered the University of California, 1968, his total income was $3,000. Before I was old enough to carry a rifle, he made his living and ours hunting in the forests and swamps along the Yazoo River in Mississippi the way his Choctaw ancestors always had. We children would wake up each morning to coonskins tacked to a shed wall to dry, and there would be alligator sandwiches about which no one spoke. Later, in California, at eight years old I killed my first bird with a slingshot, watching as a small, round stone crushed the back of a thrush's head and the bird fell with a soft, dead weight. I had no conscious purpose in killing the thrush and could never, to save my childish soul, have explained why I did so, tossing the bird carelessly into the brush afterwards. Hindsight today tells me that my purpose that day was the same purpose that drives a kitten to stalk and tumble a feather or strand of yarn. Like the kitten, I was practicing to be a serious killer when my time came. I had selected my ammunition carefully and stalked the thrush with all the skill I could muster, making no sound, blending with the surrounding manzanita and scrub oak, until I was close. Not long after the thrush, I owned a bee-bee gun and brought death to sparrows, linnets, blue jays, quail, and doves and a sad number of other birds and lizards. We ate the quail and doves, and sometimes the other birds as well, but most of my killing was a terrible, harsh wastefulness for which I am ashamed these years later, practice killing that would enrage me were I to witness it today. Then my brother, two years older, and I both acquired twenty-two rifles, and we hunted rabbits, putting to use the skills we had honed on small birds. We were now real hunters, and every day during the proper season we brought home rabbits, often five each day—shot through the head, gutted and skinned where they died—and our family ate them, often having no other food in the house. After school and on weekends and during summers, we worked the tomato and beet fields and bucked hay and built fences on ranches and with our earnings bought shotguns and deer rifles. Then we hunted quail and doves the right way, and band-tail pigeons, and deer, bringing everything home to be eaten. A handful of quail was a snack, a harvest of pigeons a family dinner; a deer, of which there were many, lasted longer even in our hungry house. We stalked and devoured the world around us, hunting and killing and eating, wasting nothing during those more mature years. Not once did I feel the killing I did was wrong; it was as thoughtless and natural as plucking an apple from a tree. Furthermore, my brother and I had crucial roles within the family. We provided sustenance from hillside and brushy river bottom.

For a while as a teen I hunted with a bow, a fifty-five-pound Bear recurve that constituted my only gesture toward sport hunting. I stopped, however, when one day I pinned a rabbit to a tree and watched the little thing spin in crying circles around the arrow shaft. Rabbits do cry in pain, and deer do scream. If you've heard either, you do not forget, and you never want to hear such a thing again. To shoot and eat a rabbit was proper and necessary. But to inflict unnecessary pain and the horror that came with it was wrong and immoral.

I have not hunted, have not shot an animal, since I left home for college and, while I was away, my mother sold all my guns. It wasn't malicious or even thoughtless; the family, with six children still at home, simply needed money in a hurry, as was often the case. But my mother's act changed my life, no doubt. Perhaps I would have stopped hunting anyway, given the different world I was entering. In college I knew no one else who hunted, knew no one who did not think hunting was a barbaric act, no one who could understand how a family might not be able to live without killing and eating the wild animals around them. This was the late sixties, early seventies, and we were all supposed to love life in a flowery sort of way, to enjoy bean curd and sprouts, to abjure killing and embrace free love, an exchange I was quite willing to make. A small town kid cast into an alien world, I would not have tried to impress my values upon my new friends even if I had thought success possible. Who was I to defend a way of life I had never questioned or even pondered? Very likely I would have drifted away from hunting anyway, but without guns that possible drift became a definite destination.

After college, I became a Wilderness Ranger for the U. S. Forest Service where, during the fall, I patrolled the High Hunt, that anomalous season in which men climbed on horseback into the high country of the North Cascades, above timberline, to kill deer and bear and mountain goats. During the high hunt, I saw the dark underbelly of killing for sport, killing done by men for no other purpose than the killing itself. I was awakened in my tent one morning by a too-close rifle shot and crawled outside to find a gut-shot bear cub squalling heart-breakingly a few yards beyond my camp, a Seattle hunter nearby with his expensive rifle. The bear cub was not legal game, but the cub had to be dispatched. The man had wanted a bearskin, and the little cub had looked immense to his urban eyes, the same eyes that had failed to notice my blue tent near his target. In Seattle the man dined on much better fare than bear meat, and the fine he paid for his error did not affect his lifestyle. On another day, I found two hunters at the end of a trail, preparing to climb into their truck with the head, horns, and cape of a mountain goat. The rest of the goat had been left behind, in violation of the law, because the hike out had been difficult and they had no interest in the meat. They wanted the trophy and could easily purchase much better cuisine than stringy goat flesh. Nobody, one of the men explained, really eats that stuff. Eons before, a man might have greatly valued a bear skin or a mountain goat's head and horns, and might have honored and even danced with such a signifier—in an act much like love—to demonstrate his ability to provide for his family and community, and his gratitude to the animal that had given itself to him so generously. But somewhere along the generations, the thing that signaled a man's ability to provide, and that man's kinship with the natural world, had become merely a trophy, a meaningless signifier of destruction.

One afternoon during that same season, deep inside that same Cascade wilderness, I had looked up to find a cougar poised on the crest of a snow ridge above me, her soft gold outlined against a pale blue sky. The cat studied me a hundred yards below her, ponderous and loud with my seventy-pound pack and red rain parka, her face a study in concentration. Obviously she had paused in mid-stride, having seen me just before I saw her, and it seemed just as obvious that certain questions were playing in her cat mind. Aware of possible problematic answers to such questions, and in no mood to be dined upon, I raised my ice axe high above my head to suggest that was someone of significance, a creature of dimension too great to be toyed with. After holding me in her quiet regard for what seemed minutes but must have been seconds, she turned and vanished with great dignity over the ridgeline. Unlike those city hunters, with their gut-shot bear cub and wasted mountain goat, the cougar had no need for a trophy and understood her world perfectly. She had granted me the consideration due something foreign and potentially valuable or dangerous, and after due regard had gone on with the serious business of life, leaving me standing absurdly alone in the mountains with ice axe aloft. If the encounter had gone differently, she might well have killed me and eaten me with only the slightest difficulty, and her action would have been proper and correct from any objective point of view not my own. Unlike that lion, the trophy hunters had no place in the moral world of the Cascade wilderness, or in any moral world. In her regard such killers would have been a mere corruption of the earth.

Today I live in the Manzano Mountains in New Mexico, on the edge of the Cibola National Forest. A dozen yards beyond our kitchen window hangs a bird feeder beneath which cottontail rabbits come to graze on blue jay spillings. Some mornings four or five of the plump cottontails crowd one another beneath the feeder, and I tease my daughters with the possibility that one weekend when I'm alone I'll go into competition with the owls and hawks and coyotes and bobcats and foxes and I'll eat those juicy bunnies. My daughters, who have had pet bunnies playing in their bedrooms, become only mock angry because they know I won't really kill and eat the rabbits. They don't know me as a hunter. That was another life. In all the time they've known me, I've killed nothing, not even a gopher. But the truth is that I simply cannot look at those cottontails without imagining them frying in butter, lightly floured, delicious. It's hard to shake old habits of thought, old instincts born of necessity.

My daughters are right of course; I won't eat the wild pets that feed and frolic outside our windows. I don't need to. We have chicken in the freezer, ground beef for the burgers we have once a month or so, a round steak to chop up when green chili stew is nec essary, tofu for those difficult diners—all from a local grocery. I fly fish with barbless hooks in trophy trout waters and release every fish because I'm told I must (not because I think it is a morally superior act), and I buy cod and salmon from the market. But still, I have a running argument with my wife and daughters. If we are not to be vegetarians, I argue, we should raise chickens so that we don't have to buy chickens or eggs from a store. Perhaps I should take up deer hunting again, I suggest, maybe elk or antelope as well. We are irresponsible, I argue, letting others do the killing for us. Worse than irresponsible, immoral, for by subsidizing the meat industry we subsidize the most horrific forms of cruelty. As a teen I worked on chicken ranches and I know these places where chickens are raised a hundred thousand at a time in long, dark buildings, fed hormones and antibiotics, never allowed sunlight, never allowed to know any life except a brief, dank prelude to death. With cattle—creatures I have helped brand, castrate, dehorn, and butcher—it is worse. And with the intelligent pig it is worse still on the massive hog farms where they live in squalor and vilely pollute the environment prior to their squealing factory deaths. If we raised chickens, the way my family did when I was a child, they could roam and scratch in the dirt, flirt with one another, fight, worry about hawks and bobcats, make love, and live full chicken lives until the day they became food for us. We would grant them dignity and they would feed us, a satisfactory exchange. If I hunted deer, the animals would live their lives in full dimension up to the very moment those lives ceased, and I would once again join the ranks of the cougar and coyote, and now, in the Southwest, the reintroduced Mexican gray wolf, as a predator. Together we would ensure our mutual dignity, the deep regard of hunter and hunted. Surely my bullet would be quicker than the coyote's slashing canines, but it would be no more humanitarian, for is it possible to think that nature has not, over countless millennia, prepared the deer to meet its coyote or cougar death, or readied the rabbit for the owl? Such death must be sacramental, a matter of mutual knowledge and the most profound respect. How else may the owl or bobcat find the rabbit except by way of the most complete knowledge possible, and what is knowledge if not respect? What is such complete knowledge and respect but a kind of love?

There is no angry god out among the trees and beside the streams where deer walk and wait for the cougar. The Creator can have no shame even in the face of a futile, heroic struggle of a doe for the life of her fawn. True understanding does not bring a metal fly rod case down on a rock to shatter the most natural reciprocity between predator and prey. This is my body, nature says, this my blood. A necessary agony and resurrection in sinew and leaf. He who loves this world is, in heart, a tracker and hunter, can be nothing else.

I cannot but think, however, that the Creator is angered and shamed by humanity's killing machines and factories, its growth hormones and pesticides and herbicides flowing from blood to blood. By our irresponsibility.

# MEAT

## Stephen J. Bodio

*How, given the canine teeth and close-set eyes that declare the human animal to be a predator, had we come up with the notion that oat bran is more natural to eat than chicken?*

—Valerie Martin, THE GREAT DIVORCE

My life has been built around animals and books about them. They have been in every book I've written and most of my essays. I was imprinted on the *Jungle Book* and Peterson's *Field Guides* before I was four, fated to be a raving bibliophiliac as long as I lived. I fed myself a constant diet of books with animals—Darwin, Beebe, Lorenz on the one hand, Kipling, Seton, Terhune, Kjelgaard on the other. I read bird guides like novels and novels about pigeons. As long as I can remember I kept snakes, turtles, insects, pigeons, parrots, fish; bred them all, learned falconry and dog training, kept life lists, raced pigeons, hacked falcons for the Peregrine Fund, did rehab, joined conservation groups, supported veterinarians, partnered for life with bird dogs. I would say I "loved" animals but for the fact the word is so worn out in our culture that I distrust it. Valerie Martin again: "... a word that could mean anything, like love. At dinner last night Celia had said, 'I love pasta. I love, love, love pasta,' and then to her father who had cooked the pasta for her, 'And you Dad, I love, love, love you.'") Suffice it to say that some animals are persons to me as well as points of focus, subjects of art, objects of awe, or quarries.

And yet? I eat meat, and always will. Which today is not only becoming vaguely suspect in some civilized quarters but also might be one point of dissension with what I understand of Buddhism. Although I also take a quote from a modern Buddhist everywhere I wander about this subject—at a bookstore, Gary Snyder once grinned as I handed him my copy of *Turtle Island* to autograph, opened to the poem "One should not talk to a skilled hunter about what is forbidden by the Buddha."

I recently announced too loudly at a dinner that I would no longer write anything with the purpose of convincing anyone to do anything. If writing essays means anything to me it is as an act of celebration and inquiry, like, if lesser than, poetry and science. With that in mind, let this be an inquiry into meat and, as my late friend Betsy used to say of the Catron County Fair, "a celebration of meat." I will try to be honest, even if it means admitting to crimes. Maybe this is about love after all.

Personal history does shape us all. I was born to blue-collar stock in the postwar suburbs. My mother's people were Irish and Scottish and English and German. Some had been farmers, one a revolutionary, and many had been fishermen, but by the time of my birth they had escaped the land and become respectable, things my animal-obsessed intelligence rejected without analysis. McCabes tended to react with disgust to the messier parts of life. I still remember with delight my outspoken little sister Anita, who used to help me clean game, when she came to visit me with our grandmother and found me making a study skin from a road killed woodpecker. She was all of eleven at the time, when many little suburban girls think they must be fastidious, but she scooped up the carcass and tossed it in the wastebasket. "You'd better get that covered up," she giggled, "or Nana McCabe's gonna puke all over the kitchen floor."

But the Bodios, who came over from the Italian Alps in their and the century's late teens, were from another planet than the lace-curtain Irish. My father had a furious drive toward WASP respectability, but his folks were Italian peasants who happened to live in Boston. Less than ten miles from downtown, they maintained until the ends of their long lives what was almost a farm. I believe their Milton lot contained half an acre's space. On it they had twelve apple trees, grapevines, and a gigantic kitchen garden. They also kept a few pigeons and rabbits. (No chickens—even then, Americans objected to the happy noise that half the planet wakes up to.)

Nana McCabe could cook pastries and cakes, but the Bodios *ate*. Eggs and prosciutt' and Parmesan, young bitter dandelions and mushrooms picked almost anywhere, risott' and polenta that, when I was very young, would be garnished with a sauce I learned ("don't tell nobody") was made from *uccelini*, "little birds"—I suspect sparrows, bushwhacked in the pigeon house. Eels and mussels—which, back then, had to be gathered rather than bought. I tasted real vegetables there, not like the canned ones at home—tomatoes and corn eaten in the garden, warm from the sun, with a shaker of salt, zucchini and eggplant soaked in milk, breaded, and fried in butter like veal. Tart apples, stored in the cool cellar where Grandpa kept his homemade wine. That wine, served at every meal, to kids and adults alike.

And, of course, meat, interesting meat. My father hunted and fished and kept racing pigeons, but has always been indifferent to food. I suspect that, until his own old age, he found his parents' food too "ethnic," too reminiscent of the social barriers he wore himself out trying to transcend. As for my mother, she hated game—the mess of cleaning and its smells, the strangeness of its taste. She passed this down to most of the kids; my sister Wendy so abhorred the idea of venison that my brother and I would tell her steak and veal were "deer meat" so we could get her portion, a sub-terfuge so effective that she would leave the kitchen, claiming to be nauseated by the imagined smell.

So the good stuff often went to the Bodios by default. *Really* good stuff—black ducks with a slight rank taste of the sea, ruffed grouse better than any chicken, white-tailed deer that would hang swaying in the garage until the meat formed a dry crust and maybe a little mold. Bluefish, too rich ("fishy") for my mother's taste, and fifty-pound school tuna.

I don't know if my parents ever realized that I, tenderest minded and softest and most intellectual of their kids, was also the one being trained to the delight of strange food, strange meat, even if the eating of it conflicted with my other "principles." My father would snap a pigeon's neck without a thought if it was too slow in the races, but he wouldn't eat it. I would cry when he "culled" (never "killed") a bird, then eat it with delight at my grandparents'.

I thought then that I was weird, and felt guilty. Now I think it's my father who was weird, and my tender-minded sisters, who would be vegetarians if they had to kill their meat. They "love" animals, de-plore my hunting. Only one of the six of them keeps animals, which are messy and take work to keep and know.

All these as-yet-unexamined attitudes and preferences came with me when I left home at seventeen. I became *seriously* weird at that point—to my parents, of course, because I grew my hair long and cultivated a beard and disagreed with them on sex, religion, politics, drugs, and money—but also, to my surprise, to many of my new friends. They of course shared my beliefs about all of the above. But at that time I usually lived in freezing shacks in seaside outer suburbs like Marshfield, with trained hawks and my dad's old .410 and 16-gauge shotguns, and "lived off the land" in a way rather unlike that of rural communards. I spent so much time in the salt marshes that one girlfriend called me, not without affection, "Swamp Wop."

I shot ducks and geese all fall, gathered mussels and quahogs and soft-shell clams. You could still free-dive for lobsters then without being assaulted by legions of vacationing boat thugs. Squid swarmed in the summer and would strand themselves in rock pools on the spring tides. In summer we—my uncivilized blue-collar workmates and I, not my friends who agreed with me on art and politics—would use eelskin rigs and heavy rods to probe for stripers in the Cape Cod Canal. Winter would find us on the sandbars, freezing but happy as we tried for a late-season sea duck for chowder or an early cod on a clam bait for the same.

Gradually I achieved some small notoriety—not just as some sort of nouveau primitive, but also as a guy who could serve you some serious food. In the late seventies I was a staff writer for a weekly postcounterculture paper in Cambridge and began to introduce occasional animal and/or food pieces to its pages. We had entered the age of debate on these subjects, but I still had fun. Just before the paper died, the food writer Mark Zanger, who still writes under the nom-de-bouffe "Robert Nadeau," and I were going to do a game dinner extravaganza, to be titled "Bodio Kills It, Nadeau Cooks It," complete with appropriate wines and between-the-courses readings from my game diary. But the owners folded the paper and I left for New Mexico, a more hospitable ecosystem for my passions.

I present the above as a partial recounting of my bona fides, but also to present you a paradox. America and American civilization are still "new" compared to, say, France, Italy, China, Japan. The movement against meat and the "Animal Rights Movement" are largely a creation of American or at least Anglo-Saxon culture, which doesn't have the world's richest culinary tradition, to say the least.

My friends considered me a barbarian, yes, but also a cook.

France and Italy and China (and even Japan—fish, after all, is meat, the "meatless" Fridays of my youth notwithstanding) eat *everything*. They eat frogs and snails, eels and little birds, dogs and cats (and yes, deplorably, tigers and bears), snakes, whales, and poisonous puffer fish. They actually eat less bulk of meat than our sentimental in-denial culture of burger munchers, but they are in that sense more carnivorous—or omnivorous—than we are.

People who eat strange meat are considered "primitive" by our culture, whether or not theirs has existed longer than ours, or created better art and happier villages.

So are our oldest ancestors, hunter-gatherers, who eat thistles and birds and eggs and grubs, roast large game animals and feast on berries like the bears they fully realize are cousins under the skin. Hunter-gatherers know animals are persons, and eat them.

Can it be that we are the strange ones? We, who use up more of the world's resources than anyone, even as we deplore the redneck his deer, the French peasant his *grive*?

Can it be entirely an accident that in the wilds of southern France the wild boar thrives in the shadow of Roman ruins? That carefully worked-out legal seasons for thrushes exist alongside returning populations of griffon vultures, lammergeiers, peregrines? That you can eat songbirds in the restaurants and look up to see short-toed eagles circling overhead? Just over the border, in Italy, they still have wolves, while in wilderness-free England and Brussels, Euromarket bureaucrats try to force the French to stop eating songbirds.

Three years ago I spent a month in the little Vauclusien village of Serignan-de-Comtat. Animals and books brought me there—in this case, the insects and books of the great Provençal naturalist and writer Jean-Henri Fabre.

The Fabre project didn't come off. But upper Provence finally gave me a template, or maybe a catalyst, to crystallize my disconnected thoughts about nature, eating, wild things, and culture into a coherent form.

The thing is: I had expected insects, sure; stone medieval villages, good food, wine and vines, lavender and broom, Roman ruins and the signs of long occupancy of the land.

I hadn't expected anything like "the wild." But on my first walk into the dry oak hills behind the town I looked up into the brilliant yellow eyes of a hovering short-toed eagle, a *circaete de Jean-le-Blanc* bigger than an osprey, with the face of an owl and long dangling legs. The snake eater soon proved common, as did red kites, almost extinct in Great Britain. A week or so later I was hiking on the flanks of Mont Ventoux in a landscape that reminded me enormously of the Magdalenas at home when I saw a soaring hawk suspended over the deep valley between me and the next ridge. This one resolved in my binoculars into the extremely rare—but returning—Bonelli's eagle, a sort of giant goshawk.

More evidence of the paradox kept coming in through the month. Restaurants, like the Saint Hubert—it was named after the patron saint of hunters—sold boar and duck; the proprietor told me to come back in the fall and eat *grives,* "thrushes." A nature magazine discussed the reintroduction of griffon vultures west of the Rhône. Birders directed me to the bare stone teeth of the Dentelles, south of Ventoux, where the bone-breaking lammergeier or bearded vulture was nesting. I didn't think they existed any longer west of the Himalayas! I caught a jazz concert in the Théatre Antique, a Roman theater in Orange, in continuous use since before the time of Christ. I looked down from wild hills with sign of badgers and foxes and deer into the ordered lines of vineyards.

Then came the morning at dawn when I surprised the two middle-aged men in camo fatigues loading their two hounds into the back of a Deux Chevaux. They replied curtly to my cheery *"Bonjour,"* but I was fascinated. *"Je suis un chasseur Americain,"* I began: I'm an American hunter . . .

The transformation was instantaneous; they both shook my hand and began speaking over each other in quick French made even tougher to understand by their heavy local accents. "You're *American,* that's good. . . . We thought you were from Paris . . . those northerners, they think they're better than us. They don't hunt, they hate hunters . . . they are all moving down here to their summer houses." I felt like I was in New Mexico. Then I caught, "Did you see the boar, M'sieur?"

I must have looked skeptical, because they led me to its track in a mud puddle across the path. The soil hadn't even settled from the water; the great beast (its tracks were huge) must have crossed the path just seconds ahead of me.

They hung around to show me game waterers to allow the animals to drink during the dry summer months, to invite me to share a *pastis* at the bar in town, to ask me to return in the fall when we could eat truffles and partridge and *bartavelle* (a kind of chukar) and *grives* and boar. I realized that, unlike in England and Germany, *everybody* hunts in France—the butcher and baker and mechanic as well as the local personages. Maybe it's the French Revolution, maybe the Mediterranean influence. I doubt that the sign on the tank, posted by my new friends and their fellow members of the Serignan hunters' society, would have appeared in England or Germany or the United States: NATURE EST NOTRE CULTURE: "Nature is our culture, our garden."

Nature *is* our culture. Our "permaculture," if you will; something a part of us, that we're a part of. Nobody in rural southern France is ignorant of what food is, or meat.

I had been trying to live something like this for as long as I had been conscious. I hunted, and gathered, and gardened, and liked it all. I spent my rather late college years in rural western Massachusetts, put a deer in the freezer and cut cordwood, some of which I sold to professors. I ate road kill for two years, cruised the roads at dawn for carcasses of cottontails and snowshoe hares and squirrels, praising whatever gods when I found a grouse (I barely had time to hunt except during deer week), learning you could cook snake and make it good. I even ate a road-killed hawk once—it was delicious.

But the French visit gave me a more coherent vision. Having confessed to one crime (yes, road kill picking is generally illegal), I'll tell you of a worse one. Or—no, let me tell this in the third person.

A naturalist recently returned from France awoke one fall morning to find his rowan trees full of hundreds of robins feeding on the red berries. He went to feed his goshawk and found the cupboard bare. But the season hadn't started.

He thought long—well, maybe five minutes—about France and food and his hungry hawk. Opened the window. The robins flew up, then returned to their gobbling.

Robins are true *grives,* "thrushes" of the genus *Turdus.* In the fall they grow fat on fruit.

He tiptoed to the gun room, got out an accurate German air rifle, cocked it, loaded it. Stood inside the open window, in the dark of the room. Put the bead on a fat cock's head and pressed the trigger. One thrush fell, the rest fled to the higher trees. He walked out, collected the fallen bird, admired its lovely colors, felt its fat breast. Made sure the pellet had passed through the head, took it to his gos's mews, where she leaped on it with greedy delight.

Now, though, he's *really* thinking. He gets down his copy of Angelo Pellegrini's *The Unprejudiced Palate* and reads, "People now and then complain that their cherries, raspberries, strawberries are entirely eaten by the birds. . . . When this is true, the offending songsters should be captured and eaten." Well, he hardly considers the robins to be "offending," but they certainly were eating fruit. Pellegrini adds that they are "delectable morsels unequaled by any domestic fowl or larger game bird." Hmmm . . .

He goes to his copy of Paul Bocuse, which features a dozen recipes. He likes the one that adds sautéed potato balls and garlic to the briefly roasted whole thrushes.

He goes back to the window. Fires six times. Six times a bird falls; six times the others flee for a moment, then return to their feasting.

He plucks them, but leaves the head, feet, and innards. Roasts them in a 425-degree oven for ten minutes. Combines them with the potatoes and sautéed garlic. Shares them with his wife, a kindred spirit, accompanied by a red Italian wine.

He tells me that they were delicious and that he doesn't feel guilty at all.

Delicious, of course. Food should be delicious, and inexpensive, and real; the last two keep it from being mannered or decadent. My hunting and gathering and husbandry are driven both by principle and by pleasure—why should they not be driven by both? But because the "good people" in our northern Protestant civilization-of-the-moment are so often gripped by a kind of Puritanism even as their opposite numbers rape the world with greed (did I write "opposite"? I wonder . . .), most writers do not write of the sensuous pleasure of food. Okay, a few: M. F. K. Fisher, first and always; Patience Gray; Jim Harrison; John Thorne. But even they don't write enough about the pleasure of *meat*. So before we return full circle to principle, to guilt and remorse, to "why," let's take a moment to celebrate the delights of our subject.

If we weren't supposed to eat meat, why does it smell so good? Honest vegetarians I know admit they can be forced to drool by the sweet smell of roasting birds. No food known to humans smells quite as fine as any bird, skin rubbed with a clove of garlic, lightly coated with olive oil, salted, peppered, turning on a spit over a fire . . .

Why do we Anglo-Saxons overcook our meat? Another residue of Puritanism, of fear of the body, of mess, of eating, of realizing that death feeds our lives? Do we feel that guilty about not photosynthesizing?

Nobody could tell me that wild duck tastes "of liver" if they cooked it in a five-hundred-degree oven for fifteen or twenty minutes.

No one could say that venison does, if they dropped thin steaks into a hot skillet, turned them over once, and removed them and ate them immediately.

Hell, nobody could tell me that *liver* tastes "like liver" if they did the same, in bacon fat, with onions already well cooked piled around it.

A cowboy I know used to say he hated "nasty old sheep." We changed his mind when we bought a well-grown lamb from the Navajos, killed and skinned and gutted it, and let it soak for a day in a marinade of garlic, honey, chilis, and soy sauce, turning it frequently. Then Omar and Christine, Magdalena's prime goat and lamb roasters, cooked the legs and ribs over an open fire, until a crust formed over the juicy interior. The smell could toll cars passing in the street into Omar's yard. Omar and I, especially, are known to stab whole racks of ribs off the grill with our knives and burn our mouths, moaning with pleasure.

Stock: I put all my bird carcasses in a big pasta pot with a perforated insert. I usually don't add vegetables. I cook them for ten to sixteen hours, never raising the stock to a boil . . . *never.* The result perfumes the house, causes shy friends to demand to stay for dinner, ends up as clear as a mountain stream but with a golden tint like butter. Then you can cook the risott' with it. But you only need a little—the real stuff uses more wine or even hot water, and a lot of Parmesan.

I love my pigeons, but have you ever eaten "real" squab, that is, five-week-old, fat, meltingly tender pigeon? I keep a few pairs of eating breeds for just that. You could cut it with a fork.

How about real turkey, the wild kind? It actually tastes like bird, not cardboard, and has juice that doesn't come from chemical "butter." Eat one, and you'll never go back.

How about the evilest meats of all, the salted kind? How about prosciutt', with its translucent grain and aftertaste like nuts? How about summer sausage? Old-style hams with a skin like the bark of an oak? How about real Italian *salame,* or *capicolla*?

Good things could be said about vegetables, too, by the way. We here at the Bodio household actually eat more vegetables than meat; meat is for essence and good gluttony, not for bulk. We eat pasta and rice and beans, cheese, good bread, garden vegetables by the ton, roasted vegetables, raw ones. But these things don't need a defender. Meat, improbably to me, does.

Let's veer in through that sensuousness once more. Last month I was preparing five domestic ducks for a feast with friends. To cook it the best way the breast meat had to be blood rare, the legs well done with a crispy skin. Which of course involved totally dismantling the ducks, hard work. You had to partly cook them, then skin them, getting seriously greasy. (The skin would become crackling, or as Libby called it, punning on the pork-crackling *chicharonnes* of New Mexico, "pata-ronnes.") You had to fillet the breast meat from the bone, and disjoint the legs. The carcasses had to go back into the oven for browning, and then into the stockpot. You ended up physically tired, sweaty, with aching hands, small cuts everywhere, and slime to your elbows. You felt good, accomplished, weary. But it was hard to avoid the idea that you had cut up an animal, or five.

Or take a *matanza*, a pig killing, in Magdalena. After shooting the pig in the head (if you do it right, the other pigs watch, but nobody, not even the hero of the feast, gets upset), it's work, work that will give you an appetite. The pig is carried out on a door, wrapped with burlap sacks, boiled in one half of a fifty-gallon drum, scraped, hung up. It is eviscerated, and the viscera are washed and saved. The bulk of the "real" meat, all that will not be eaten that day, goes to the freezer. The *chicharonnes* are cut up and heaped into the other half of the drum, to sizzle themselves crispy in their own fat. Everything steams in the cold air—the fires and vats, your breath, the pig's innards. Those innards are quickly fried with green chilis and wrapped in fresh flour tortillas so hot they'll burn your tongue, to give you energy to rock that carcass around, to stir the *chicharonne* vat with a two-by-four. The blood is taken in and fried with raisins ("sweet blood") or chilis ("hot blood") and taken out to where you are working. By afternoon you are as hungry as you have ever been. You eat like a wolf. You also can't avoid the idea that you have taken a life. Afterward you all lie around like lions in the sun.

I once mentioned a *matanza* in a piece I wrote for the Albuquerque *Journal*. An indignant letter writer (from Massachusetts!) called me "refuse" for my "Hemingwayesque" love of "blood, hot and sweet," which he assumed was a grim metaphor rather than a rural delicacy. He hurt my feelings. But maybe he was right, in a way he hadn't intended.

So, okay, *death*. And cruelty.

Deliberate cruelty is inexcusable; I won't say much about it here. As I get older I actually use bigger calibers and gauges than when I was young; I can't stand wounding anything.

But death? We all cause it, every day. We can't not. Tom McGuane once said, "The blood is on your hands. It's inescapable." Vegetarians kill, too . . . do they seriously think that farming kills nothing? Or maybe they're like the Buddhist Sherpas that Libby used to guide with, who would ask her to kill their chickens and goats so the karma would be on *her* hands.

Let me pause for a moment to quote from two yet-unpublished books, books that might find publishers more easily did they not reject a lot of current foolishness. From Allen Jones's *A Quiet Violence*, a philosophical investigation of hunting: "The vegetarian does have good intentions. He or she is making an honest attempt to relate more directly to the natural world. The irony, of course, is that in denying their history they have placed themselves farther away from the process. . . . When death is seen as evil, or if pain is something to be rejected at all costs, then nature itself is in danger. If most animal rights activists had their utopias, neither ecology nor evolution would exist."

And from Mary Zeiss Stange's forthcoming *Woman the Hunter*: "Far from being a mark of moral failure, this [hunter's] absence of guilt feelings suggests a highly developed moral consciousness, in tune with the realities of the life-and-death process of the natural world."

An acceptance of all this is not always easy, even for the hunter and small farmer, who usually know animals far better than the vegetarian or "anti" or consumer. I find that as I get older, I am more and more reluctant to kill anything, though I still love to hunt for animals, to shoot, and to eat. Still, I am determined to affirm my being a part of the whole mystery, to take personal responsibility, to remind myself that death exists, that animals and plants die for me, that one day I'll die and become part of them. "Protestant" "objectifying" "northern" culture—I use those quotation marks because none of those concepts is totally fair or accurate, though they do mean something—seems to be constantly in the act of distancing itself from the real, which does exist—birth, eating, juicy sex, aging, dirt, smells, animality, and death. Such distancing ends in the philosophical idiocies of the ornithologist Robert Skutch, who believes sincerely that God and/or evolution got the universe wrong by allowing predation and that he, a Connecticut Yankee, would have done better.

I, on the other hand, don't feel I know enough about anything to dictate to the consciences of others. I certainly don't think that anyone *should* kill, so long as they realize they are no more moral than those who do; I can find it hard enough myself. While I suspect the culture would be saner if we all lived a bit more like peasants, grew some vegetables out of the dirt, killed our own pigeons and rabbits, ate "all of it" like bushmen or Provençal hunters or the Chinese, I have no illusions that this is going to happen tomorrow. I can only, in the deepest sense, cultivate my garden, sing my songs of praise, and perfect my skills. I'll try to have what Ferenc Maté calls "a reasonable life," strive to be aware and compassionate and only intermittently greedy, to eat as well as my ancestors, to cook well and eat well as a discipline and a joy. The French say of a man who has lived well that *"Il bouffe bien, il boit bien, il baise bien"*: "He eats well, he drinks well, he [in this context] fucks well." Sounds like a life to me.

And in living my good and reasonable life, I suspect I should sometimes kill some beautiful animal and eat it, to remind myself what I am: a fragile animal, on a fierce fragile magnificent planet, who eats and thinks and feels and will someday die: an animal, made of meat.

# THE PIPAL PANI TIGER

## Jim Corbett

BEYOND THE FACT that he was born in a ravine running deep into the foothills and was one of a family of three, I know nothing of his early history.

He was about a year old when, attracted by the calling of a chital hind early one November morning, I found his pug marks in the sandy bed of a little stream known locally as Pipal Pani. I thought at first that he had strayed from his mother's care, but, as week succeeded week and his single tracks showed on the game paths of the forest, I came to the conclusion that the near approach of the breeding season was an all-sufficient reason for his being alone. Jealously guarded one day, protected at the cost of the parent life if necessary, and set adrift the next is the lot of all jungle folk; nature's method of preventing inbreeding.

That winter he lived on peafowl, kakar, small pig, and an occasional chital hind, making his home in a prostrate giant of the forest felled for no apparent reason, and hollowed out by time and porcupines. Here he brought most of his kills, basking, when the days were cold, on the smooth bole of the tree, where many a leopard had basked before him.

It was not until January was well advanced that I saw the cub at close quarters. I was out one evening without any definite object in view, when I saw a crow rise from the ground and wipe its beak as it lit on the branch of a tree. Crows, vultures, and magpies always interest me in the jungle, and many are the kills I have found both in India and in Africa with the help of these birds. On the present occasion the crow led me to the scene of an overnight tragedy. A chital had been killed and partly eaten and, attracted to the spot probably as I had been, a party of men passing along the road, distant some fifty yards, had cut up and removed the remains. All that was left of the chital were a few splinters of bone and a little congealed blood off which the crow had lately made his meal. The absence of thick cover and the proximity of the road convinced me that the animal responsible for the kill had not witnessed the removal and that it would return in due course; so I decided to sit up, and made myself as comfortable in a plum tree as the thorns permitted.

I make no apology to you, my reader, if you differ with me on the ethics of the much-debated subject of sitting up over kills. Some of my most pleasant shikar memories center round the hour or two before sunset that I have spent in a tree over a natural kill, ranging from the time when, armed with a muzzle-loader whipped round with brass wire to prevent the cracked barrel from bursting, I sat over a langur killed by a leopard, to a few days ago, when with the most modern rifle across my knees, I watched a tigress and her two full-grown cubs eat up the sambur stag they had killed, and counted myself no poorer for not having secured a trophy.

True, on the present occasion there is no kill below me, but, for the reasons given, that will not affect my chance of a shot; scent to interest the jungle folk there is in plenty in the blood-soaked ground, as witness the old gray-whiskered boar who has been quietly rooting along for the past ten minutes, and who suddenly stiffens to attention as he comes into the line of the blood-tainted wind. His snout held high, and worked as only a pig can work that member, tells him more than I was able to glean from the ground which showed no tracks; his method of approach, a short excursion to the right and back into the wind, and then a short excursion to the left and again back into the wind, each maneuver bringing him a few yards nearer, indicates the chital was killed by a tiger. Making sure once and again that nothing worth eating has been left, he finally trots off and disappears from view.

Two chital, both with horns in velvet, now appear and from the fact that they are coming down-wind, and making straight for the blood-soaked spot, it is evident they were witnesses to the overnight tragedy. Alternately snuffing the ground, or standing rigid with every muscle tensed for instant flight, they satisfy their curiosity and return the way they came.

Curiosity is not a human monopoly: many an animal's life is cut short by indulging in it. A dog leaves the verandah to bark at a shadow, a deer leaves the herd to investigate a tuft of grass that no wind agitated, and the waiting leopard is provided with a meal.

The sun is nearing the winter line when a movement to the right front attracts attention. An animal has crossed an opening between two bushes at the far end of a wedge of scrub that terminates thirty yards from my tree. Presently the bushes at my end part, and out into the open, with never a look to right or left, steps the cub. Straight up to the spot where his kill had been he goes, his look of expectancy giving place to one of disappointment as he realizes that his chital, killed, possibly, after hours of patient stalking, is gone. The splinters of bone and congealed blood are rejected, and his interest centers on a tree stump lately used as a butcher's block, to which some shreds of flesh are adhering. I was not the only one who carried fire-arms in these jungles and, if the cub was to grow into a tiger, it was necessary he should be taught the danger of carelessly approaching kills in daylight. A scatter-gun and dust-shot would have served my purpose better, but the rifle will have to do this time; and, as he raises his head to smell the stump, my bullet crashes into the hard wood an inch from his nose. Only once in the years that followed did the cub forget that lesson.

The following winter I saw him several times. His ears did not look so big now and he had changed his baby hair for a coat of rich tawny red with well-defined stripes. The hollow tree had been given up to its rightful owners, a pair of leopards, new quarters found in a thick belt of scrub skirting the foothills, and young sambur added to his menu.

On my annual descent from the hills next winter, the familiar pug marks no longer showed on the game paths and at the drinking places, and for several weeks I thought the cub had abandoned his old haunts and gone further afield. Then one morning his absence was explained, for side by side with his tracks were the smaller and more elongated tracks of the mate he had gone to find. I only once saw the tigers, for the cub was a tiger now, together. I had been out before dawn to try to bag a serow that lived on the foothills, and returning along a fire track my attention was arrested by a vulture, perched on the dead limb of a sal tree.

The bird had his back towards me and was facing a short stretch of scrub with dense jungle beyond. Dew was still heavy on the ground, and without a sound I reached the tree and peered round. One antler of a dead sambur, for no living deer would lie in that position, projected above the low bushes. A convenient moss-covered rock afforded my rubber-shod feet silent and safe hold, and as I drew myself erect, the sambur came into full view. The hind quarters had been eaten away and, lying on either side of the kill, were the pair, the tiger being on the far side with only his hind legs showing. Both tigers were asleep. Ten feet straight in front, to avoid a dead branch, and thirty feet to the left would give me a shot at the tiger's neck, but in planning the stalk I had forgotten the silent spectator. Where I stood I was invisible to him, but before the ten feet had been covered I came into view and, alarmed at my near proximity, he flapped off his perch, omitting as he did so to notice a thin creeper dependent from a branch above him against which he collided, and came ignominiously to ground. The tigress was up and away in an instant, clearing at a bound the kill and her mate, the tiger not being slow to follow; a possible shot, but too risky with thick jungle ahead where a wounded animal would have all the advantages. To those who have never tried it, I can recommend the stalking of leopards and tigers on their kills as a most pleasant form of sport. Great care should however be taken over the shot, for if the animal is not killed outright, or anchored, trouble is bound to follow.

A week later the tiger resumed his bachelor existence. A change had now come over his nature. Hitherto he had not objected to my visiting his kills but, after his mate left, at the first drag I followed up I was given very clearly to understand that no liberties would in future be permitted. The angry growl of a tiger at close quarters, than which there is no more terrifying sound in the jungles, has to be heard to be appreciated.

Early in March the tiger killed his first full-grown buffalo. I was near the foothills one evening when the agonized bellowing of a buffalo, mingled with the angry roar of a tiger, rang through the forest. I located the sound as coming from a ravine about six hundred yards away. The going was bad, mostly over loose rocks and through thorn bushes, and when I crawled up a steep bluff commanding a view of the ravine the buffalo's struggles were over, and the tiger was nowhere to be seen. For an hour I lay with finger on trigger without seeing anything of the tiger. At dawn next morning I again crawled up the bluff, to find the buffalo lying just as I had left her. The soft ground, torn up by hoof and claw, testified to the desperate nature of the struggle, and it was not until the buffalo had been hamstrung that the tiger had finally succeeded in pulling her down, in a fight which had lasted from ten to fifteen minutes. The tiger's tracks led across the ravine and, on following them up, I found a long smear of blood on a rock, and, a hundred yards further on, another smear on a fallen tree. The wound inflicted by the buffalo's horns was in the tiger's head and sufficiently severe to make the tiger lose all interest in the kill, for he never returned to it.

Three years later the tiger, disregarding the lesson received when a cub (his excuse may have been that it was the close season for tigers), incautiously returned to a kill, over which a zamindar and some of his tenants were sitting at night, and received a bullet in the shoulder which fractured the bone. No attempt was made to follow him up, and thirty-six hours later, his shoulder covered with a swarm of flies, he limped through the compound of the Inspection Bungalow, crossed a bridge flanked on the far side by a double row of tenanted houses, the occupants of which stood at their doors to watch him pass, entered the gate of a walled-in compound and took possession of a vacant godown. Twenty-four hours later, possibly alarmed by the number of people who had collected from neighboring villages to see him, he left the compound the way he had entered it, passed our gate, and made his way to the lower end of our village. A bullock belonging to one of our tenants had died the previous night and had been dragged into some bushes at the edge of the village; this the tiger found, and here he remained a few days, quenching his thirst at an irrigation furrow.

When we came down from the hills two months later the tiger was living on small animals (calves, sheep, goats, etc.) that he was able to catch on the outskirts of the village. By March his wound had healed, leaving his right foot turned inwards. Returning to the forest where he had been wounded, he levied heavy toll on the village cattle, taking, for safety's sake, but one meal off each and in this way killing five times as many as he would ordinarily have done. The zamindar who had wounded him and who had a herd of some four hundred head of cows and buffaloes was the chief sufferer.

In the succeeding years he gained as much in size as in reputation, and many were the attempts made by sportsmen, and others, to bag him.

One November evening, a villager, armed with a single-barrel muzzle-loading gun, set out to try to bag a pig, selecting for his ground machan an isolated bush growing in a twenty-yard-wide *rowkah* (dry watercourse) running down the center of some broken ground. This ground was rectangular, flanked on the long sides by cultivated land and on the short sides by a road, and by a ten-foot canal that formed the boundary between our cultivation and the forest. In front of the man was a four-foot-high bank with a cattle track running along the upper edge; behind him a patch of dense scrub. At 8:00 p.m. an animal appeared on the track and, taking what aim he could, he fired. On receiving the shot the animal fell off the bank, and passed within a few feet of the man, grunting as it entered the scrub behind. Casting aside his blanket, the man ran to his hut two hundred yards away. Neighbors soon collected and, on hearing the man's account, came to the conclusion that a pig had been hard hit. It would be a pity, they said, to leave the pig for hyenas and jackals to eat, so a lantern was lit and as a party of six bold spirits set out to retrieve the bag, one of my tenants (who declined to join the expedition, and who confessed to me later that he had no stomach for looking for wounded pig in dense scrub in the dark) suggested that the gun should be loaded and taken.

His suggestion was accepted and, as a liberal charge of powder was being rammed home, the wooden ramrod jammed and broke inside the barrel. A trivial accident which undoubtedly saved the lives of six men. The broken rod was eventually and after great trouble extracted, the gun loaded, and the party set off.

Arrived at the spot where the animal had entered the bushes, a careful search was made and, on blood being found, every effort to find the 'pig' was made; it was not until the whole area had been combed out that the quest for that night was finally abandoned. Early next morning the search was resumed, with the addition of my informant of weak stomach, who was a better woodsman than his companions and who, examining the ground under a bush where there was a lot of blood, collected and brought some blood-stained hairs to me, which I recognized as tiger's hairs. A brother sportsman was with me for the day and together we went to have a look at the ground.

The reconstruction of jungle events from signs on the ground has always held great interest for me. True, one's deductions are sometimes wrong, but they are also sometimes right. In the present instance I was right in placing the wound in the inner forearm of the right foreleg, but was wrong in assuming the leg had been broken and that the tiger was a young animal and a stranger to the locality.

There was no blood beyond the point where the hairs had been found and, as tracking on the hard ground was impossible, I crossed the canal to where the cattle track ran through a bed of sand. Here from the pug marks I found that the wounded animal was not a young tiger as I had assumed, but my old friend the Pipal Pani tiger, who, when taking a short cut through the village, had in the dark been mistaken for a pig.

Once before when badly wounded he had passed through the settlement without harming man or beast, but he was older now, and if driven by pain and hunger might do considerable damage. A disconcerting prospect, for the locality was thickly populated, and I was due to leave within the week, to keep an engagement that could not be put off.

For three days I searched every bit of the jungle between the canal and the foothills, an area of about four square miles, without finding any trace of the tiger. On the fourth afternoon, as I was setting out to continue the search, I met an old woman and her son hurriedly leaving the jungle. From them I learnt that the tiger was calling near the foothills and that all the cattle in the jungle had stampeded. When out with a rifle I invariably go alone; it is safer in a mix-up, and one can get through the jungle more silently. However, I stretched a point on this occasion, and let the boy accompany me, since he was very keen on showing me where he had heard the tiger.

Arrived at the foothills, the boy pointed to a dense bit of cover, bounded on the far side by the fire track to which I have already referred, and on the near side by the Pipal Pani stream. Running parallel to and about a hundred yards from the stream was a shallow depression some twenty feet wide, more or less open on my side and fringed with bushes on the side nearer the stream. A well-used path crossed the depression at right angles. Twenty yards from the path, and on the open side of the depression, was a small tree. If the tiger came down the path he would in all likelihood stand for a shot on clearing the bushes. Here I decided to take my stand and, putting the boy into the tree with his feet on a level with my head and instructing him to signal with his toes if from his raised position he saw the tiger before I did, I put my back to the tree and called.

You who have spent as many years in the jungle as I have need no description of the call of a tigress in search of a mate, and to you less fortunate ones I can only say that the call, to acquire which necessitates close observation and the liberal use of throat salve, cannot be described in words.

To my great relief, for I had crawled through the jungle for three days with finger on trigger, I was immediately answered from a distance of about five hundred yards, and for half an hour thereafter—it may have been less and certainly appeared more—the call was tossed back and forth. On the one side the urgent summons of the king, and on the other, the subdued and coaxing answer of his handmaiden. Twice the boy signaled, but I had as yet seen nothing of the tiger, and it was not until the setting sun was flooding the forest with golden light that he suddenly appeared, coming down the path at a fast walk with never a pause as he cleared the bushes. When half-way across the depression, and just as I was raising the rifle, he turned to the right and came straight towards me.

This maneuver, unforeseen when selecting my stand, brought him nearer than I had intended he should come and, moreover, presented me with a head shot which at that short range I was not prepared to take. Resorting to an old device, learned long years ago and successfully used on similar occasions, the tiger was brought to a stand without being alarmed. With one paw poised, he slowly raised his head, exposing as he did so his chest and throat. After the impact of the heavy bullet, he struggled to his feet and tore blindly through the forest, coming down with a crash within a few yards of where, attracted by the calling of a chital hind one November morning, I had first seen his pug marks.

It was only then that I found he had been shot under a misapprehension, for the wound which I feared might make him dangerous proved on examination to be almost healed and caused by a pellet of lead having severed a small vein in his right forearm.

Pleasure at having secured a magnificent trophy—he measured 10'3" over curves and his winter coat was in perfect condition—was not unmixed with regret, for never again would the jungle folk and I listen with held breath to his deep-throated call resounding through the foothills, and never again would his familiar pug marks show on the game paths that he and I had trodden for fifteen years.

# Part Nine

*I'd sooner, except the penalties, kill a man than a hawk.*

—Robinson Jeffers
"HURT HAWKS" (1928)

# COMMUNION

## Dan O'Brien

I'M OLD ENOUGH to remember rows of headless chickens hanging by their bound feet from the clothesline in our back yard. I can still smell the wet feathers being peeled away by human hands, and a familiar childlike wonder continues to well up in me when I think of the coils of steaming intestines stripped from those avian body cavities. Probing those intestines with a stick shed from the huge walnut tree in our back yard may have been the nudge that sent me down the road of biological inquiry, love of wildness, and deep appreciation for the natural world.

It is not a coincidence that I am also of the last American generation that can remember life before television. I recall my father's proclamation when he and my uncle wrestled the enormous box with the tiny, nine inch, green screen into the living room. "It's just a fad," my father said. "It will never amount to anything." True to his reputation for guileless wisdom my father turned out to be at least half right.

Television may not ever have amounted to anything but what did amount to something was the experience my father gave me that same year.

It must have been 1958 or '59 when I raised a two hundred and fifty pound 4H hog from a forty-pound piglet. In the late summer I had out-scurried a pack of gritty ten year olds to secure a prime oinker in the annual greased pig chase at the county fair. My father, who was a dairy man at heart, embraced the project of growing the pig to butchering size on a diet of many pounds of beautiful, fragrant, yellow corn, a little alfalfa hay and plenty of pure water.

I was not raised by a bunch of Buddhists. It was understood from the get-go that my hog would one day grace our table in the form of bacon, ham, and pork chops. I helped take care of the hog, of course, and like any ten year old, toward the end I was struggling to understand why my pig had to die. My father, who had never heard of pantheism, explained it with a thoughtful squint. "Everything dies," he said. Then, after a hesitation, he added more to himself than to me, "But nothing is really lost."

Only in later years did I come to know what he meant. That hog of mine was once a bunch of corn growing in a field near where my granddad is buried. Part of it might have been my grandfather. By the next winter my hog was part of me.

My father not only didn't see himself as a pantheist, he fancied himself a Presbyterian. "It's a sin to kill without a good reason," he said, "but putting a hog on the table is a good reason. Might even be a sacrament." Still, I wasn't sure about killing my hog. I lobbied for keeping my hog and just going to the grocery and buying ham and bacon, but my father shook his head. He took this moment to teach a life-lesson. "We take responsibility for what we do," he said. It is a lesson I've tried never to forget.

When I talk about killing, one thing must be understood: killing for the sake of killing is not a good reason. It should not be tolerated in any form. Faux-hunters who shoot animals to see if they can hit them, the teen-ager who swerves the car to run over the raccoon, even children who stone frogs in play need to be discouraged, chastised, shunned, and finally prosecuted by the greater society. What they have done is clearly as far beyond their rights as the activities of the mouse-trapper, the fly swatter, the hunter, the farmer, the shopper, the normal human being, are within their rights.

Sometime not long after my experience with the 4H hog I became possessed by a love of the arcane lifestyle of falconry. I use the world lifestyle because words like pastime, sport, or recreation measure only one surface of the prism that is falconry. Viewed from one angle falconry can supply access to the biology of both predator and prey. Another view illuminates the complexities of wind and weather. Physics plays a part. The intangibles of instinct and courage are ever present. Falconry is fresh air, clear skies, honest exercise. It gives the practitioner an avenue to interrelate with other species on a meaningful and intimate level. It is intimately intertwined with the realities of survival, conditioning, evolution, and, of course, killing.

There are many reasons to take a falcon to the field. When I pick my falcon up from her block, hood her, and start out with the setters racing ahead I expect to be thrilled by the beauty of the landscape, I expect to be challenged or caressed by the wind. I expect communion with the natural world of which I am part. I also expect that, if there is any killing that day, it will adhere to the criteria set down by my father: there must be a good reason and I must accept responsibility for what I've done. In the case of falconry the reasons for killing are manifold. First, both the falcon and I eat what she kills. Second, I enjoy watching, and learn from the aerial maneuvers of both predator and prey. By taking the time to train a falcon to trust me, I am able to observe what few humans are blessed to observe; the simple everyday interaction between a falcon and her prey.

On a good day it goes something like this: we leave the house on foot, after the work is done, when the sun is well into its downward slide. The pointing dogs streak ahead of me, running too fast, disappearing over one hill and reappearing from behind the next with worried faces, wondering what is slowing the falcon and me. I'm walking with the falcon on my fist toward a field where prairie chickens can often be found at this time of day. We're hunting the wild cousins of those birds that were butchered behind the house when I was young but these birds have not been compromised by captivity. Prairie chickens are smart and strong. Their instincts make them very difficult to catch. They require a lot of killing.

When I get to the part of the pasture where I can overlook perhaps ten square miles of prairie I signal the dogs to hunt and off they go, heading right to the place that we all know is most likely to hold prairie chickens. The young dog runs in a beeline, but the old dog is wiser. He swings down wind so he will be able to scent the birds when he is still eighty yards away. He is the first to set up solid, his tail high and still as a flagpole. The puppy stops when he sees the older dog pointing, mostly in anticipation of the flush he knows will be coming, but partly out of sheer admiration.

I wait a beat to be sure that the dogs are sure and then I take the hood off the falcon's head. She narrows her black eyes on the horizon and rouses her feathers straight. She sees the dogs and knows what the granite in their stance means to her. She lets the wind suck her off my fist and begins an upward spiral as I make my way up wind of the dogs. By then she is a black anchor shape eight hundred feet above me, the dogs, and the prairie chickens that she believes are there.

I flush the birds and when they careen off we all know that the poorest one will die. The falcon folds and drops. Drops, drops, curving first with the wind then across it, to a volume of air that is shared with a prairie chicken. On the best days the strike is so efficient that it appears to be amiss. But the prairie chicken tumbles from the sky and falls dead on the floor of the Great Plains.

As natural as a falcon's flight might be, my father's second criterion still must be met. I am not delusional enough to deny my part in the death of that prairie chicken. Had I not tamed the falcon, trained the dogs, flushed the bird at just the right time, there would have been no kill. Sure, if the falcon had been fully wild she would have killed that day, perhaps multiple times. There is no doubt that she enjoys killing, that every evolutionary twist has honed her skills, that she is a natural killer. But still, on the days that I take her forth, I am the choreographer, it is my needs and desires that are fulfilled and I must shoulder that responsibility.

To honor that responsibility I try to make sure that the prey is not killed ignobly by the falcon (who, of course, could not care less about the nobility or ignobility of the prairie chicken's death). If the prairie chicken reaches cover fairly I do not send the dogs in to reflush it. I try to call the falcon back if it looks like she might kill it on the ground. And if the prairie chicken does die, I let the falcon eat her fill and take the remains back for my own table. I bury the head or the heart of the bird as a thank you and offering to whatever God makes all those marvelous wheels turn. But I don't shirk my duty; I don't pretend that I am above the killing of animals. I accept my place within the animals of this earth, not above them like so many of my contemporaries do.

In the winter of 2000 I drove from Los Angeles to Santa Barbara. It is a drive through land thousands of times more fertile than the land I am used to and as a couple friends and I wound our way north through the shagged, poisonous, blanket of humanity that has been laid over the coast of Southern California I wondered at the animal populations that have been displaced to create the sprawl of Los Angeles, Malibu, Ventura, and up along the ocean's edge to Santa Barbara. But the popular word "displaced" is a euphemism for the more accurate word "killed." As any biologist knows, animal populations do not simply move. With few exceptions, if they could live in a different area they would already be there. No, the populations of animals, from aphids to grizzly bears, are gone. Killed as surely for human desires and needs as I kill prairie chicken on the Great Plains. But, of course, we are not talking about individuals whose importance to the species is almost non-existent. We are talking about populations of creatures, attacked not on the individual level but on the habitat level. It was sad to think of all those animals that were killed, but sadder to think of all those people pretending they had nothing to do with it.

We cruised through Oxnard and I, the only professed killer in the car, was the only one to notice that nothing lives in Oxnard, nothing survives in that most fertile of soils and gentlest of climates except broccoli, cauliflower, Swiss chard, and garlic for the tables of people with hands scrubbed as clean of blood as denial and pretense will allow.

The people of Santa Barbara, like the people of any city, indeed any place in the United States and beyond, might well have been shocked to know that a killer had slipped past the town limits. But only the truly ignorant ones could look me in the eyes and rail against my grasp of life, because anyone who has given it any honest thought knows that for all the shortcomings of people like me, at least we step up to the plate and take responsibility for who we are and what it means to be human. We do not pretend that our existence is benign.

We do not let the arrogance of specific hierarchy delude us into thinking we are something other than another animal among many. Those who deny the identity I embrace commit an act deeper and sadder than the denial of culture, race, religion, or family. A denial like that is sadder than the man who changes his name from Avram Horiwitch to Andy Horton. Sadder than a college friend of mine who spent two nights a week straightening her beautiful African hair. Shame on them and shame on the forces that make them consider it.

In market places in South America and in Africa I have seen chickens hanging by their feet that remind me of those birds on the clothesline in my childhood back yard. Sometimes they still wore their heads, sometimes their horny feet were still intact, usually there was a patch of feathers somewhere on the birds to guarantee to the housewives who bought them that these were indeed chickens of the Earth and that they had been killed honestly for the consumption of humans of the Earth. The women I met in those countries would never have bought a completely naked chicken presented to them under a film of plastic. They did not need insulation between themselves and killing, they could accept responsibility for the killing they caused. And I'm the same. I'll continue to take my falcon to the field and bring back to my table what he leaves for me. I know where I come from and I will not turn my back on who I am.

# THOUGHTS ON KILLING

## Charles Fergus

AT THE END of one unusually successful day, I plucked two grouse on the edge of our meadow, leaving the feet and the heads for the scavengers. My son, five years old at the time, happened upon the scatter of pretty feathers. I was working at some other task outside, and had an immediate pang when I saw him pick something up. As I approached, I saw his face knotted up. He looked at me, a grouse leg in one hand, a head in the other.

I can't remember my exact words, but we talked about killing. I told my son that whatever we do, we end up taking life. Living arises from killing, new life from the ashes of death. To eat, we are forced to kill—something. I tried to explain that even planting a field was an act that caused death, through banishment of the creatures that originally lived in the brush or the grass that was abolished to make the field. Whatever we do, I told my son, we affect the world. The pang I had felt when seeing him was sadness in knowing that he must come to an understanding of how the world functions—an understanding that includes the realization that he himself will not abide on the earth forever.

The source of our living is something that many modern people wish to keep in the background. Theirs, as T. H. White put it, is "an abstract world where water is an idea that comes out of a tap, and light a conception in a switch." And where food, I would add, is a perquisite gotten from a shelf in boxes or cans, or plastic-wrapped from a display case. At times, I have been condemned by vegetarians for my hunting. I wonder if they count the number of worms, beetles, flies, spiders, mice, rabbits, sparrows, and hawks whose habitat is destroyed by the fields of vegetables, the deserts of soybeans. I can kill a bird, then go back the next year and flush another one from the same place.

But there's no denying it: Killing is an integral part of the hunt. As the philosopher Ortega has noted, "One does not hunt in order to kill; on the contrary, one kills in order to have hunted." The whole intricate, difficult ritual comes to fruition in the moment that the prey is slain. Some have written that if they could bring down a bird without killing it, in the same manner that a fisherman can land a trout without harming it, they would never kill another. To me this sounds like an affected piety, at best a conceit not fully thought through.

Archie Carr, a naturalist from Florida, writes, "Almost from birth I have been peculiarly tormented by Jekyll-and-Hyde compulsions both to learn about the natural history of animals and to eat them." For me, no such guilt exists. Which is not to say that I do not feel an elegiac, almost a weary sadness when a bird, formerly vibrant and cunning, lies inert in my hands. But the skillful shooting exonerates the killing, as does the dog in her great joy, as does the preparing and eating of the game, themselves acts of veneration. Cleaning a bird, I marvel at the mechanics of its body, the overlay of feathers, the limbs and appendages well suited to certain modes of living (the grouse's fringed snowshoe feet and the duck's ruddering paddles, the woodcock's worm-gripping bill). Eating a bird, I savor it twice: I taste the succulent flesh, and I remember how I brought it to bag. After the meal I boil the carcass for soup. I strain out the bones and scatter them in the woods, or, if there's a hot fire in the stove, toss them in and burn them. The ash is spread on my garden in the spring.

Probably I sound more convinced than I really am in describing my feelings about killing. I am never fully certain that what I do is correct. I somehow think that doing as much of life's killing myself is better than paying someone else (whether slaughterer or farmer) to do it by proxy. Sometimes I wonder if animals have souls. My dog, I believe, has one. It would not surprise me if the grouse who drove his bill into Jenny's eye had a soul. But there is in me a savage joy that even the thought of life-taking and soul-extinguishing cannot put down. I take my chances. I kill swiftly, eat what I slay, and keep the knowledge of my own death close at hand.

# Contributors

ERNEST HEMINGWAY (1899–1961) was arguably the greatest American writer of the twentieth century. *For Whom the Bell Tolls* (1940), his best-selling novel of the Spanish Civil War, may not have been his finest book, but in its imagery of love and death was certainly his most powerful, with set-piece scenes like El Sordo's stand on the hilltop, Pilar's monologue on the slaughter of the Fascists, and their subsequent retaliation, and Pilar, again, describing the smell of death. The passage excerpted here is more contemplative. It discusses in brief, humorous dialogue a difference of opinion between the novel's central character, the intellectual American volunteer, Robert Jordan, and his peasant guide, a soft-hearted hunter named Anselmo. They disagree, in a quiet, genteel, Cervantes-like way, about the propriety of the killing of men as against the killing of animals. Its understated humor conceals a very serious point.

ERICH MARIA REMARQUE (1897–1970) was the author of the internationally best-selling antiwar novel *Im Westen Nichts Neues (All Quiet on the Western Front)*, based on his experiences as a German infantryman in the murderous trenches of World War I. *All Quiet* was followed three years later by *The Way Back* and *Three Comrades,* set in Weimar Germany. Remarque's books were among the thousands ordered destroyed by Hitler in the infamous book burnings of 1933. Non grata in Nazi Germany, Remarque moved to France and later to Switzerland, where in 1946 he completed another bestseller, *Arch of Triumph.* His 1954 novel, *A Time to Love and a Time to Die,* dealt with World War II on the Eastern Front, and the situation in the German homeland under Hitler's rule. This chapter from *All Quiet,* which I first read when I was 14, has stuck with me for more than half a century. Nowhere else in literature, I feel, is the personal horror of war—the killing of one man by another, face to face—expressed with more power.

JOHN JAMES AUDUBON (1785–1851) was America's foremost bird artist, his fame based largely on the life-sized elephant quarto *Birds of America,* completed in 1838. The paintings need no description: they are everywhere. But Audubon was also a keen if self-trained naturalist, and his five-volume *Ornithological Biography* of 1839, which was meant to complement the bird paintings with words, makes fascinating reading even today, interlarded as it is with asides about the long-gone people, mores, and frontier society he met along his way.

Many people today think Audubon painted his birds "from life." Not so. He painted them from death. In those days before cameras and high-speed film, a wildlife artist had to kill the creatures he studied before he could paint them. Audubon needed a bird in hand to catch its true colors, proportions, and the details of its feathering. In the course of his career he killed thousands of them, ranging from hummingbirds to eagles, including such now-extinct species as the Passenger Pigeon—his description of their slaughter by market hunters and farmers, who often fattened their pigs on the overkill, is a classic in the literature of American natural history and is included here. He was an excellent marksman with both shotgun and rifle, though some of his avian targets inevitably flew off wounded and irretrievable. He mourned their loss, as much for the pain he'd caused them as at the missed opportunity to get on with his artwork. Birds he wounded but retrieved he often kept in a cage while he was painting them, and then released them back to the wild. The Audubon who emerges from his journals was neither a St. Francis of Assisi nor a bloodthirsty game hog. Rather he appears as a dedicated artist, a self-critical man, somewhat vain and competitive (particularly with his arch-rival Alexander Wilson), often humorous and sharp-tongued in his observations of human behavior, and a loving husband and father who missed his wife and children deeply while he was in the field—often for eight months at a time. Yet reading between the lines, one can see that the French-born Audubon shared his native culture's enthusiasm for comely women regardless of his marital vows. All rather quaint and poignant by today's dubious standards . . .

In 1843, at age 58 already an old man by the standards of the day, he embarked up the Missouri River on what was to prove his last long research trip. He was planning to produce a book called *Viviparous Quadrupeds of North America,* which he hoped would do for the continent's mammals what his earlier work had done for its birds. The West in those days was still quite wild, fraught with dangers from Indians, rattlesnakes, drought, and sudden storms. He completed the trip successfully but never lived to finish the book. In 1851, in the 66th year of his age, he died as a result of a stroke suffered four years earlier. His son John completed it.

ALDO LEOPOLD (1886–1948), the twentieth century's most influential voice for an American "land ethic," an issue still unresolved in the new millennium, worked for the U.S. Forest Service and taught courses in game management at the University of Wisconsin. Shortly before his death, fighting a grass fire on a neighbor's property in 1948, he had become an advisor on conservation to the United Nations. His *Sand County Almanac* (1949) dealt mainly with life on his hardscrabble farm in the glacier-scoured countryside of central Wisconsin. But it also carried essays on Leopold's hunting experiences in the Southwest, during his Forest Service days, the most powerful of which is included here. No one has captured the remorse a hunter feels after a misguided kill more poignantly than in Aldo Leopold's image of "the green fire dying." Read it, but don't weep. Just think before you shoot.

DAN GERBER, born and bred in western Michigan but a citizen of the world in the broadest sense, is one of America's finest poets. He has worked as a corporate executive, an automobile dealer, a professional racing driver (until a high-speed collision with the exit wall at Riverside, California, in 1966), and more prosaically in later years, a high school and college teacher. From 1968 through 1972, with Jim Harrison, he co-edited the literary magazine *Sumac.* In addition to six books of poetry, most recently *Trying to Catch the Horses* (1999), he is also the author of three highly-praised novels, *American Atlas* (1973), the gritty racing novel *Out of Control* (1974), and *A Voice from the River* (1990), much of which is set in New Guinea during World War II. His short story collection *Grass Fires,* published in 1987, is reminiscent of Sherwood Anderson's *Winesburg, Ohio,* but in my estimation much better. Winner of the 1992 Michigan Author Award and a nominee for a Pushcart Prize, his work was selected for *The Best American Poetry: 1999.* He's also the recipient of the Society for the Study of Midwestern Literature's "Mark Twain Award" for 2001, joining such company as Wright Morris, William Gass, William Maxwell, and his friend Jim Harrison.

I've known Dan since 1973, made two long East African safaris with him, fished and hunted with him until he hung up his shotgun, which is the subject of his original essay for this book, "Some Thoughts on Adam's Curse." For a number of years we met each Memorial Day to attend the Indianapolis 500, from which Dan's non-fiction book *Indy: The World's Fastest Carnival Ride* (1978) derived, replete with wild, grim, funny action pix by *Sports Illustrated* photographer Heinz Kluetmeier, a longtime mutual friend of ours. Dan and I even share yellow Labrador retrievers who are littermates, my Jake and his Willa (as in Cather). Dan and his wife Debbie, an avid horsewoman, divide their year between central California and southeastern Idaho. A new, wide-ranging collection of his essays, *A Second Life,* dealing with his adventures from the high Arctic to the sports car tracks of the Southwest and Elkhart Lake, Wisconsin, will appear this year from Michigan State University Press.

JIM HARRISON, outdoorsman, poet, novelist, screen writer, and outspoken essayist, is the author of seven novels and four novella collections, most recently *The Beast God Forgot to Invent* (Atlantic Monthly Press), the essay collection *Just Before Dark,* seven collections of poetry, and the children's book, *The Boy Who Ran to the Woods.* A keen upland bird hunter and a world-class cook and eater of wild game, he nonetheless has longstanding qualms about killing that tastiest of game birds, the woodcock. These reservations are best expressed in this chapter from his third and perhaps finest novel, *Farmer* (1976). Harrison lives most of the year in northern Michigan and winters in southern Arizona.

ROBERT F. JONES has written seven highly acclaimed novels (*Deadville, The Buffalo Runners, Blood Tide, Blood Sport, Blood Root, Slade's Glacier,* and *The Run to Gitche Gumee*) and five works of nonfiction, among them *Dancers in the Sunset Sky*. His novel *Blood Tide* was named a New York Times Notable Book in 1990. And *Blood Sport* has achieved cult status as one of the finest, wildest, and first novels of magical realism. A frequent contributor to *Men's Journal, Sports Afield, Outdoor Life,* and *Big Sky Journal,* and an editor at large for *Shooting Sportsman Magazine,* his articles, short stories, and essays have also appeared in *Audubon, Time, Sports Illustrated, Life, People, Harper's Fly Rod and Reel,* and *The New York Times.* His work has appeared in twenty-two book-length anthologies, among them *Best American Sports Writing.* An outdoorsman for more than fifty years, Mr. Jones has hunted and fished to greater or lesser effect throughout New England, the Middle West, the Far West, the South, the Caribbean, Mexico, Costa Rica, Europe, and East Africa. He lives with his wife, Louise, in Vermont, along with two gundogs, a wild-eyed cat named Spike Jones, and countless flyrods, books, and shotguns.

LEO TOLSTOY (1828–1910). Count Lev Nikolaevich Tolstoi was the titan of the nineteenth-century novel. *War and Peace* (1865–1868) is considered by many to be the greatest novel ever written, followed closely by *Anna Karenina* (1874–1876). Both novels range far and wide, high and low, through Russian and European society and the psychology of their day, coming to grips with most of the social problems of the period. They delve deeply into human nature, as exemplified by their huge casts of fascinating characters. But Tolstoy also understood animal nature and loved the wild outdoors, as this rarely cited excerpt from *Anna Karenina* shows. Levin, the human protagonist of the episode—a snipe hunt in the Volga Steppes—is the character in *Anna* who most closely resembles its author. Laska, the canine protagonist, is Levin's eager, anxious pointer. By subtly shifting his points of view between man and dog, and then back again, Tolstoy shows, better than anyone has before or since, the tensions that exist on any hunt, the intense inter-species camaraderie, the love and fear a gundog feels for its master, and the respect both feel for their prey. It is to my mind the best bird-hunting scene in all literature.

MARY CLEARMAN BLEW is the author of the acclaimed family memoirs *All But the Waltz* (a 1991 Pacific Northwest Booksellers Award winner), and *Balsamroot.* Her other books include three short-story collections, *Lambing Out, Sister Coyote,* and *Runaway* (a 1990 Pacific Northwest Booksellers Award winner), and *Bone Deep in Landscape: Essays on Writing, Reading, and Place.* Her short fiction has appeared in the *O. Henry Prize Collection* and in *The Best American Short Stories.* She grew up in Montana and now lives in Idaho, where she is a professor of English and director of the creative writing program at the University of Idaho in Moscow.

RODERICK LANGMERE HAIG-BROWN (1908–1976) was born in England but moved to British Columbia as a young man and made his long, successful life there, as a writer, angler, logger, and jurist. The author of 25 books, he is perhaps best remembered for his memoir *A River Never Sleeps* and the tetralogy *A Fisherman's Year,* comprising accounts of his angling activities and ruminations through the four seasons. In *Fisherman's Spring* (1951), from which this chapter is taken, he makes one of the first reasoned arguments I've read for "Putting Fish Back." A master stylist in the cool British manner, yet a man of great compassion, he is considered by many to be the best writer on fishing who ever laid down his rod for a pen.

JOHN HOLT has wandered the Western outback and probed its fish-rich waters for nearly 30 years. He is the author of eleven books, among them *Knee Deep in Montana's Trout Streams* (1991), *Chasing*

*Fish Tales* (1993), and *Guide Wars* (1997). Often described as the Hunter Thompson of fly fishing, he is outspokenly anti-establishment, vehemently anti-strip-mining and clear-cutting, and an avowed enemy of the runaway Californication of his beloved northern Rockies. Yet his writing, though often outrageously opinionated—as evident in this original essay for *On Killing*, which deals with the credo of catch-and-release and what he calls "the gospel according to Barbless Hook"—is at the same time humorous, wry, and warm-hearted in all the right places. These qualities are played to strong advantage in his most recent book, *Coyote Nowhere: In Search of America's Last Frontier*, published to high praise last fall by St. Martin's Press. On their 26,000 mile road trip with fly rod and camera, John and his photographer partner, Ginny Diers, traveled, camped, fished, and just generally hung out in the northern Great Plains from Wyoming through the Dakotas and Montana, and clear up to Canada's Northwest Territories. John's essays and articles have appeared in *Fly Fisherman*, the *New York Times*, the *Denver Post*, *Men's Journal*, *Big Sky Journal*, *Audubon*, *E*, *Travel & Leisure*, *Sports Afield*, *Fly Rod & Reel*, and *Gray's Sporting Journal*, among other publications. He lives in Livingston, Montana, with Ginny Diers, his son Jack and daughter Rachel. I've known John for a dozen years, made many memorable hunting and fishing road trips with him, and count him among my closest and most valued friends. He is presently at work on a series of novels about today's West.

Isak Dinesen (1885–1962), the Danish Baroness Karen Dinesen von Blixen-Finecke, wrote three collections of eerie Gothic short stories, foremost among them *Winter's Tales* (1943), but is best remembered for the lyrical memoir of her life and loves in colonial Kenya, *Out of Africa* (1937), and its successor, *Shadows in the Grass* (1960). The posh Nairobi suburb of Karen is named for her home farm, and I have hunted wild guinea fowl on one of her former coffee plantations, now reverted to bushveldt, on the Tana River (and in turn, armed only with a 20-gauge shotgun, been hunted by Cape buffalo along its densely-forested banks). The love of her life was the English big game hunter and pioneer bush pilot Denys Finch-Hatton, who figures prominently in this passage, as do the lions they both kill, yet love simultaneously.

LE ANNE SCHREIBER taught in the Harvard English Department for three years, and then left academe to become a staff writer for *Time* magazine, where she covered foreign affairs and the 1976 Summer Olympics. That led to a stint as editor-in-chief of *Womensport's Magazine*, founded by Billie Jean King, and later to her appointment as sports editor of *The New York Times*, where she supervised a staff of fifty-nine men. In 1980, she left sports to serve as deputy editor of *The New York Times Book Review* for the next four years. In 1984, she moved from Manhattan to Columbia County, where she has worked as an independent journalist and writer of essays, memoirs, and criticism. She is the author of two memoirs, *Midstream* (Viking/Penguin 1990) and *Light Years* (The Lyons Press, 1996). Her shorter work has appeared in *Life, Glamour, Elle, Self, The New York Times Sunday Magazine,* and *The Yale Review*. She has received several awards for her writing, including the 1992 National Magazine Award for the best public interest journalism of the year. In recent years, she has taught in Columbia University's graduate writing program and at The New York State Writer's Institute in Albany.

LOUISE JONES is a frequent contributor to *Brill's Content* and *Publisher's Weekly,* where she reviews mysteries, and a senior writer and book columnist for southern Vermont's acclaimed *Stratton Magazine.* Her work has appeared in *Organic Gardening* and *Country Jour-*

*nal.* She was a fulltime bookseller for 17 years at the Northshire Bookstore in Manchester Center, Vermont, which the *New York Times* has rated one of America's eight best independent bookstores. A superb cook and gardener, she inaugurated a memorable and highly praised weekly food column, "The Eclectic Kitchen," in Westchester County's *Patent Trader.* Braised marmot was *not* one of her most popular recipes.

BERYL MARKHAM (1902–1986), author of *West with the Night* (1942), which became a best-seller when it was reprinted in the U.S. in 1983, on the heels of resurgent feminism, was born in Britain but raised in the wild Rongai Valley on Kenya's Mau Escarpment, where her father had a farm. As a girl she hunted reedbuck and boars (warthogs) with a spear, running barefoot though the thornbush with her Murani tribesmen friends Arab Maina and Arab Kosky, and her dog Buller, a cross between an English sheepdog and a bull terrier. This account of one such hunt ends tragically, but typically of Markham, expresses no regrets. She went on from this idyllic girlhood to become a professional horse trainer and Africa's first woman aviator, carried mail, passengers and freight from the Anglo-Egyptian Sudan to Tanganyika and Rhodesia, spotted elephants for professional hunter Denys Finch-Hatton's safaris in the Tsavo region, and vied with Karen Blixen (Isak Dinesen) for his love. In 1936, Markham became the first aviator of either sex to fly the Atlantic from Europe to America—against the prevailing westerlies—crash-landing in Nova Scotia when she ran out of fuel. I met her in her last years, at Nairobi's Muthaiga Club. She was still beautiful in her 80s, a hard drinker who could still hold her liquor, a terrifyingly fast driver, and an unquenchable fount of thrilling, caustic, tough, and sometimes raunchy tales of the Africa that was. During an abortive coup d'etat against President Daniel Arap Moi's government in the early 1980s, while all the other white residents of Karen were lying low for fear of flying bullets, Markham wheeled her Bentley at speed through the streets and past roadblocks, impervious to gunfire, headed for the Muthaiga Club. She was not going to miss her accustomed cocktail hour because of a silly political spat. Ah, Africa! Ah, Beryl!

PAM HOUSTON is the author of two works of fiction, *Cowboys Are My Weakness* (the 1993 winner of the Western States Book Award) and *Waltzing the Cat.* Her stories have been selected for *Best American Short Stories,* (1990, 1999), *Prize Stories: The O. Henry Awards* (1999), and *The Best American Short Stories of the Century* (1999), as well as a Pushcart Prize. Houston is the editor of the anthology, *Women on Hunting,* and has written the text for a book of photographs called *Man Before 10 A.M.* She has been a contributing editor to *Elle* and *Ski,* writes regularly for *Condé Nast Sports for Women,* and has been a guest on CBS-TV Sunday Morning with "Postcards from Colorado." Formerly a hunting guide and a river guide, she lives at an altitude of 9,000 feet in southwestern Colorado.

ALLEN MORRIS JONES moved to Montana's Missouri Breaks region with his family at the age of twelve, and published his first short story two years later. After graduating from the University of Montana with highest honors, he backpacked through Europe and hunted in Africa, where he won certification as a licensed Professional Hunter. On his return, at the age of 25, Jones was named editor of Montana's highly regarded *Big Sky Journal,* holding the post from 1995 to last year, when he stepped down to concentrate entirely on writing. He is the author of *A Quiet Place of Violence: Hunting and Ethics in the Missouri River Breaks* (1997), from which this elk-hunting episode is excerpted. Houghton Mifflin will publish his first novel, *Last Year's River*, this fall. A quiet, thoughtful man, perhaps a bit reclusive, his brooding intensity reminds me of the Breaks themselves, one of the wildest regions left in the Lower Forty Eight.

JOHN JEROME sometimes claims to be retired but can't prove it. He has in the past raced in automobiles, on skis, and in swimming pools, but now lives as slowly as possible in far western New England and writes books. He has also taught school, edited newspapers and magazines, and worked as a technical writer and advertising copywriter. A former columnist for *Esquire* and *Outside* magazines, he has been a fulltime freelance writer since 1968, publishing over two hundred magazine articles in newspapers and magazines including *The New York Times Sunday Magazine, Outside, Playboy, Harper's, Skiing, Car and Driver, The Runner, Runner's World, Running, Vogue, G.Q., Boston Globe Sunday Magazine, Science,* and *Harvard.* He is the author of thirteen books, including *Truck, Stone Work, The Elements of Effort,* and *On Turning Sixty-five: Notes from the Field.* He is currently at work on a book about dog training.

LOUIS OWENS is the author of five novels (*Bone Game, Dark River, Nightland, Wolfsong,* and *The Sharpest Sigh*) and seven books of nonfiction, including *Mixedblood Messages.* A professor of English and Native American Studies at the University of California, Davis, he has published more than a hundred critical essays and nonfiction pieces, as well as short fiction. His awards include the American Book Award, the PEN–Josephine Miles Award, a National Endowment for the Arts Fellowship, a National Endowment for the Humanities Fellowship, and a Fulbright.

STEPHEN J. BODIO, a hunter-naturalist, falconer, pigeon fancier, sometimes educator (at Sterling College's Wildbranch Writing

Workshop), inveterate traveler to the wildest corners of the world, and full-time writer, is the author of seven books, among them *A Rage for Falcons* (1984), *Querência* (1990) and *Aloft: A Meditation on Pigeons and Pigeon-Flying* (1990). This excerpt, the concluding chapter of his most recent book, *On the Edge of the Wild: Passions and Pleasures of a Naturalist* (1998), deals with the Lucullan pleasure he takes in eating wild meat, and, more subtly, his passion for everything wild. Bodio, an improper Bostonian by birth and education, lives with his wife Libby in south-central New Mexico, on the Plains of San Augustin under the loom of the Magdalena Mountains, where he has made his home since 1981. With them live a wondrous collection of gundogs, hawks, pigeons, shotguns, and rare, very readable books about nature, hunting, fishing, and everything under the sun. I have been there. It is the closest I've ever come to Merlin's cottage, as described by one of Bodio's—and my own—favorite writers, the late T.H. White, in *The Sword in the Stone.*

MAJOR JIM CORBETT (1875–1955) grew up in India when much of the subcontinent was still wild and tigers were many and murderous. As a boy, he hunted deer and game birds "with an old muzzle-loading shotgun—the right barrel of which was split for six inches of its length, and the stocks and barrels of which were kept from falling apart by lashings of brass wire—wandering through the jungles of the *terai* and *bhabar* in the days when there were ten tigers to every one that now [1944] survives." Today the Bengal tiger is endangered, on the brink of extinction. He developed a great love and respect for this largest of wild cats. In the early years of the 20th Century, Corbett—or "Carpet Sahib," as he was known among grateful villagers—was frequently called upon by District Commissioners to hunt down and kill known man-eaters. This resulted in his best-selling *Man-Eaters of Kumaon* (1946), from which this chapter is taken, and three later books about man-eaters. Following

India's independence in 1947, Corbett retired to Kenya where he wrote his last books, *Jungle Lore* and *My India*. He died at the age of 80 and was buried on the grounds of the Outspan Hotel—a grand old pile dating back to Kenya's early colonial period at the turn of this century—at Nyeri, in the heart of the Aberdare Range. Lord Baden-Powell, who gave the world the Boy Scouts, once said: "The nearer to Nyeri, the nearer to heaven." Old India hands felt that Nyeri and its cool, green environs were "the Simla Hills of Africa," in reference to the cool Himalayan foothills where the elite of the British Raj spent their summers. Baden-Powell himself is buried on the Outspan's grounds. I visited Corbett's grave at the Outspan on a trip to Kenya in 1990. It was a dark, hot night, after a dispiriting day spent seeing what poaching, overpopulation, and runaway cutting of tropical hardwoods had done to the once lush Aberdares, and over Corbett's grave I recited what seemed to me a fitting epitaph, from Edward FitzGerald's translation of Omar Khayyám's *Rubáiyát:*

> They say the Lion and the Lizard keep
> The Courts where Jamshyd gloried and drank deep:
> And Bahram, that great Hunter—the wild Ass
> Stamps o'er his Head, but cannot break his Sleep.

Then I danced a little buck-and-wing, in the style of Walter Huston in *The Treasure of the Sierra Madre,* beside Carpet Sahib's tomb. He did not stir, not even for this wild Ass.

DAN O'BRIEN is the author of three works of nonfiction: *The Rites of Autumn, Equinox,* and *Buffalo for the Broken Heart,* and five works of fiction: *Eminent Domain* (winner of the 1987 Iowa School of Letters Short Fiction Award), *Spirit of the Hills* (winner of the 1988 Western Writers Best First Novel Award), *In the Center of the Nation, Brendan*

*Prairie,* and *The Contract Surgeon* (winner of the 2000 Western Heritage Award for Best Novel). His short stories and articles have appeared in *The New York Times, Forbes FYI, Men's Journal,* and *Michigan Quarterly Review and Best American Short Stories, 1976.* He has written several screenplays and co-produced the documentary *A Falconer's Memoir,* which aired nationwide in the spring of 2000. His awards and accolades, in addition to those mentioned above, include a 2001 Bush Foundation fellowship, an honorary doctorate from the University of South Dakota: the 1988 Western Writers Best First Novel Award: several artist's grants from the National Endowment for the Arts; a 1988 Breadloaf Scholarship; and fellowships from the South Dakota Arts Council, among others. A wildlife biologist, who was instrumental in helping the Peregrine Fund bring the peregrine falcon back from the brink of extinction, O'Brien lives with his four dogs, two cats, two horses, and two peregrine falcons on his 1,700-acre ranch near the Badlands of South Dakota, where he raises buffalo and writes.

CHARLES FERGUS has hunted birds for over a quarter of a century. He is the author of *A Rough-Shooting Dog, Gun Dog Breeds,* and *The Wingless Crow,* as well as the highly praised novel *Shadow Catcher.* A full-time freelance writer, Fergus lives with his wife, son, and gundog in the Allegheny uplands of eastern Pennsylvania, in a stone house he built by himself. In this excerpt from the conclusion to *The Upland Equation: A Modern Bird-Hunter's Code* (1995), Fergus tries to explain why he hunts and kills game, both to his young son and, just as importantly, to himself. Brief though the excerpt is, I find it as carefully considered—and far more eloquent—than any single passage in Ortega y Gassett. It's a fitting summation to this anthology.